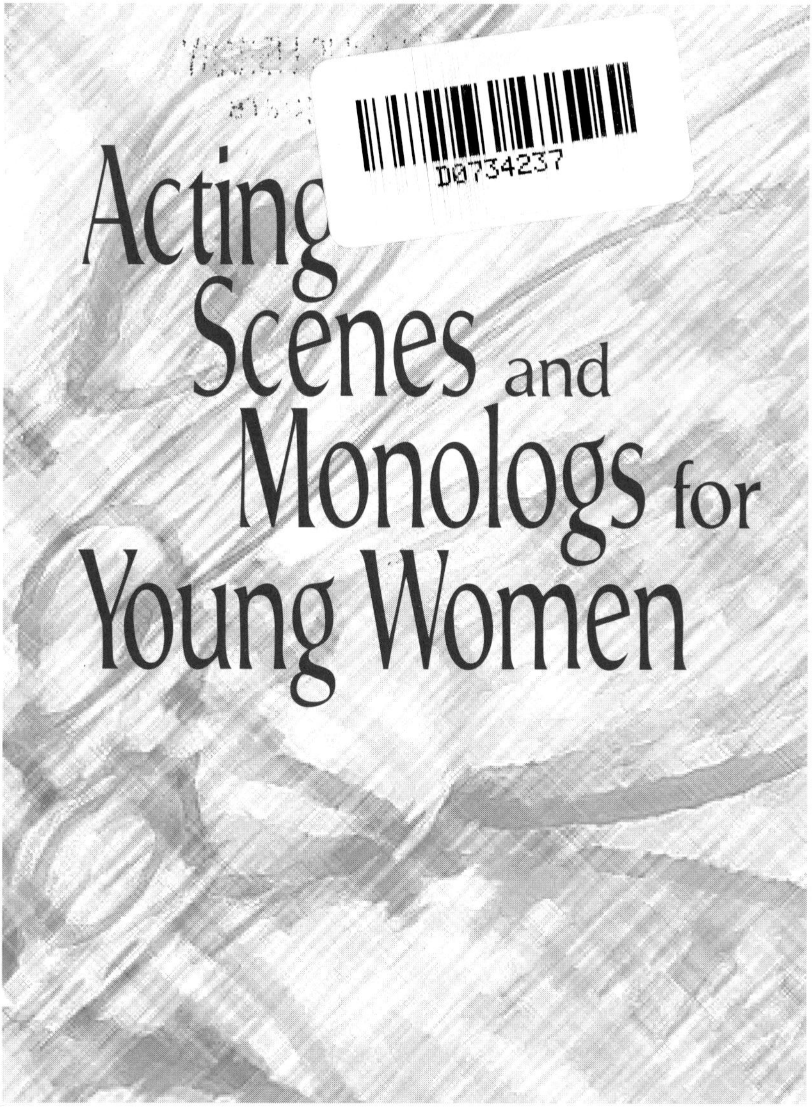

Acting Scenes and Monologs for Young Women

MAYA LEVY

MERIWETHER PUBLISHING LTD.
Colorado Springs, Colorado

Meriwether Publishing Ltd., Publisher
P.O. Box 7710
Colorado Springs, CO 80933

Editor: Arthur L. Zapel
Typesetting: Elisabeth Hendricks
Cover design: Janice Melvin

Printed in the United States of America
First Edition

Library of Congress Cataloging-in-Publication Data

Levy, Maya.
Acting scenes and monologs for young women / Maya Levy.
p. cm.
ISBN 1-56608-049-5 (pbk.)
1. Monologues 2. Acting I. Title.
PN2080.L48 1998
812'.54--dc21 98-49593
CIP

1 2 3 4 5 6 7 8 03 02 01 00 99

Dedication

To actors everywhere, who make writing for the stage such a joy. And to their teachers, their directors, who share their journey of discovery. To all the actors I've ever worked with, who, in risking all, walked with me into mystery.

Preface

These *Acting Scenes And Monologs For Young Women* are written for actors. To challenge, engage, to enjoy, no matter what the level of experience.

When working with these scenes, actors and directors should answer two questions. What's happening between the characters? What's happening with the individual character?

What the actor feels, the audience feels. What the actor sees, the audience sees. What the actor hears is heard by the audience.

Make them your own. Be experimental, play with them to see where they lead you, and above all, have a great time.

Maya Levy

CONTENTS

Monologs

Winners, Losers

I'm never going back. I'll leave the country if I have to. I'll go to Mexico, or Canada, or Ireland. I'm never going back to school again. I'll find someplace where things like this don't happen.

It was like being in a horror movie. Worse, because it was real. And unreal, at the same time. Like time stopped and something else kicked in, some special time that was slow motion, and fast forward at the same time. I know that makes no sense, but neither does anything else.

People are all over the television blathering the same old stuff. Blaming it on TV violence, or hand guns or maybe he was abused when he was three. Who wasn't? And everybody watches TV. And can get their hands on a gun. Nobody mentions that maybe the guy's just the biggest loser of the century.

The Athletic Awards are always special. We're proud of our athletes. Some people don't like sports, but I think they're important. I'm on the volleyball team, and we had a pretty good year. We had a lot of fun and I didn't gain weight or take up smoking or get drunk every weekend, like some kids do.

I'll never forget that morning, no matter how long I live or whatever else happens to me. It's imprinted on my brain like a color photograph. We were all standing around in the gym, waiting for the awards ceremony to start. Everybody was feeling good. We'd worked hard all year, and this was our chance to be recognized. We were the real winners, and this was our chance to shine.

Bobby Freedlov and I were talking about the math test we took yesterday. He didn't understand the third problem, or my explanation of how to make it work. So, I stooped down to get my calculator out of my backpack, which was on the floor, so I could show him, and ... oh Lord. Oh my God. Oh. Oh. Oh. No. No. No. No. No.

Bobby took the first bullet. Because I stooped down to get my calculator. Otherwise ...

Sammy K took the second. Then Betsy and Sal and Kevin and Ladrika and Anthony. And Latasha. And Rosa. And I don't know who else. Anthony's on the critical list. They say Kevin's paralyzed.

Before they got him, that creep shot over fifteen people. At least twenty more were injured in the stampede and panic that followed. Rosa's dead.

How come the biggest loser in school can just walk into the gym, start shooting and take down all the best. It's not fair. It'll never be fair. He thinks it makes him a big man, I guess. But it doesn't. Oh sure, he'll get a lot of attention now, and somebody'll write a book or make a movie. But he'll always be a loser.

I fell to the floor when I heard the first shot. Bobby fell on top of me. His bleeding body protected me from the rampaging crowd. I just lay there on the floor, covered with Bobby's blood, while hundreds of kids screamed and ran and nobody knew what to do. He bled to death, right on top of me. Somebody told me I was lucky.

I don't know. All I know is I'm never setting foot in school again. It's too dangerous. I'd rather go swimming with sharks than go back to school.

But, if I don't go, he wins. He has control over my life. Never. I'll never let a loser like that decide what I do or don't do, where I go or don't go. He may be the Valedictorian of Death, but I'm still alive. I may be scared, but he won't stop me.

I guess I'll have to go back to the gym too. It'll be hard. No it won't. It'll be easy. Because I'm determined to not let that loser win. I'll march right in there and ... and ... I'm going to .... to ... Well. Maybe ... Maybe not tomorrow. Maybe the gym will have to wait.

Flowers

I love flowers. Their bright colors are like songs floating on the air. And they smell so grand. Better than perfume. I just love coming to the garden center. So many wonderful plants and flowers to adore.

See that woman over there, with the overflowing cart? Buying everything she sees. Trees, shrubs, flowers. She's either a compulsive shopper or just bought a new house and needs everything.

That man by the begonias might be a scientist. He told the sales guy he needed a something or other to round out his collection. I'll bet he has all his plants labeled and cataloged like books in a library. Ficus benjamina on aisle 2, split leaf philodendron on aisle five. Poppies and pansies next to petunias and peanuts.

The lady over by the geraniums just likes to come look at all the pretty flowers. I see her here all the time. I like to look at the flowers too.

I'm searching for the perfect plant. Not too big, not too small. Can't take much sun, and has to have a flower. A pink flower, 'cause I really like pink. My garden at home was full of pink flowers. Oh, I hope the new owner waters them every day. If she hasn't pulled the whole thing out to put in a patio or hot tub.

I started my garden when I was just a kid. It's always been my garden. Dad helped me get the soil ready, but I did all the planting, watering, and weeding. I miss it. I miss my daisies, and day lilies, and petunias and impatience. I miss them a lot.

I wish Mom and I could have kept the house, but they had to sell. For the divorce settlement. Some lucky person got my garden. While

I got a tiny room in a tiny condo with no grass or flowers and one little window with just enough sunlight coming in to grow one plant.

Maybe I should buy this English ivy. Or that pothos. They're pretty hearty. Grows anywhere, and doesn't need much light. But it has no flowers. I like that rubber tree. It's nice.

I don't know why they had to get a divorce. They won't talk about it, either one of them. Something about growing apart. I always thought you grew apart for a while, then came back together to grow again, but Mom says that's not necessarily so.

We had a good life. We did things together on weekends. Went to movies, and out for pizza. Dad always took me to the ballet when it came to town. We had fun together. Now, on those few occasions I do see him, he's like a tree somebody forgot to water. All limp and brown. Mom just mopes around like a once bright geranium that's been dumped out of its pot and left there.

There's no hope really, that they'll get back together. But, we will always be a family, no matter what. No divorce paper or law or whatever can change that.

Oh look. Over there, on that table. Isn't it wonderful? It's perfect. Perfectly perfect. And I've never had a bromeliad. What a gorgeous pink blossom, sticking straight out of the center. They say that every time it blooms, it makes another plant. Two plants from one. Good. I'll divide it, and give one to Mom, and one to Dad.

No, I won't. They never were very good with plants. I'm the gardener in the family. When the time comes, I'll just buy a bigger pot.

Who Cares?

I think it looks great. *(Touches very noticeable nose ring.)* Next, I'll do my eyebrows, then my navel, then, who knows. My tongue might be, you know, impressive.

Why does she have to scream about it? — Nobody'll hire you for the summer. So. Work's for other people. An' she's wrong. Plenty of people wanna hire me. I could care less.

I'm hitting the road anyhow. Night Rider 'n me's headin' out on the Harley. LA does it for me, but he thinks Toronto's hot. Who cares. Toronto's cool.

Long way from this exercise in terror. Mom howling at the moon every night 'cause Dad dumped her for a younger chick. Who cares. Get a life, Mom. So, my brother gets busted for dealing. He's a loser. Nobody gives a hoot about him. So the dog bit the dust for playing on the white line. Cripes. There's a zillion dogs in the world. Nobody cares. Get another.

So, maybe I didn't make such hot grades. So. So. So, I got caught with that coat. So. So they booted me out. So. So. Who cares. Not me.

No way I'm stayin' in my room. Night Rider 'n me got seats tonight. No way I'm missin' The Cosmic Cavemen. They're gonna be so big one day, 'cause, 'cause they care. They really care. They care about the music, and the fans. They're the only ones that do.

Yeah. Eyebrows, navel, tongue. Brilliant.

The Most Wonderful Laugh in the World

I didn't sleep very well last night. My mom was really bad. She should be in the hospital, but she won't go and Dad wants her home. We have hospice, but still ... she's in a lot of pain. She has a blue drip in her arm, for pain. Calls it "my blue heaven."

She's so little now, so fragile. I look at her, and wonder if she's just going to vanish into the pillow overnight. I'm afraid that one morning I'll go into her room, and there'll be nothing but a little dent in the pillow, where her head used to lay.

I can't stand it. I just can't stand it.

Sometimes, when Dad doesn't think anybody's around, he'll start to cry. He was out on the patio this morning, sitting on the bench as the sun came up, sobbing his heart out. I know, because that's where I was going, to cry my heart out too.

Mom wants me at school. She wants me to live a normal life. In our house, your mother home, wasting away, is normal. All I want to do is cry. That's become normal too. Sometimes, school takes my mind off things. Sometimes.

I can't stand it. I just can't stand it. What's going to happen to me, when my mom ... when ...? I'll still have my dad. And my brothers, and Gramma and Poppy. Even so ... there's nobody like my mom. Nobody. Not in the whole world.

Know what I hate most? How I made her life so miserable, when she first got sick. I was so mean and hateful. But I was so mad, and hurt. How could she do this to me? To herself.

But nobody really does it. It just happens. Nobody would ever wish that on themselves. I don't really blame her. It's not her fault. It just happened. But why did it have to happen to her? To my mom. The best mom in the universe.

I didn't know what to do, so I took it out on her. I feel so bad about that. It made her feel so much worse, I know.

Last night, I told her how bad I feel about the awful things I did, and she said she understood, and forgives me. Now, I guess, I have to forgive myself.

I can't stand it. That she's going away. That I'll never see her again in my whole life. That we'll never laugh together. I just can't stand it! That she won't see me graduate, or get married, or ever meet my children. My little girl I'll name after her. She'll never ever see her. Never.

Dad's videotaping everything, and she looks so beautiful, even if she is so frail. She glows, with an inner light I've never seen before. She's simply gorgeous. And the funny thing is, we're having more fun together now than ever. She reads poetry to me, poems I never would have read on my own. We watch funny movies together, and giggle and laugh. She has the most wonderful laugh. So full of life and love. And joy. You know what I did? I hid my tape recorder in my pocket, and taped her laughing at some silly movie. When she's gone, I can always play my mother laughing with me, and for those few moments, we can be together again.

I can't stand it. I can't. I just can't. I CAN'T STAND IT!

Harmony

When my dad told me we were moving to the desert, I was so disappointed. I mean, we had everything. A nice house, swimming pool. We were close to the tennis courts. I went to a great school. I had a lot of friends I didn't want to leave. We all have to make sacrifices, he said, so I might as well adjust.

He's right. He had to get away from his job, and the city and all that stress. Sell our house and move to the end of the world. Because, he said, the world's gone nuts, and the only way to get away from it is to go where there aren't any people. What else can you do when you get cancer? Thank goodness for e-mail, or I wouldn't have very many friends.

Actually, I've come to love the desert. I love the prickly pears, and the cholla. The mesquite trees, and palo verde. I love walking the desert trails. A quail family comes on the patio every morning for breakfast. The lizards scoot around like crazy, and make this great rustling noise. A roadrunner comes every day, and bangs his head into the plate glass patio doors. I told him it's only his reflection in the glass, but he doesn't believe me. He thinks there's a roadrunner inside that looks just like him. He thinks it's a girl. I don't think he's too bright.

And I finally have a horse. Ruby. Not a very horsey name, but she told me that's her name. Who am I to argue with a horse?

My dad bought this hammock, to de-stress himself. Afternoons, he swings in the hammock, listening to baseball. Can't watch TV 'cause he sold the satellite. Said the news was too depressing, and all the shows too stupid to watch and there wasn't anything on unless you wanted to shop or pray.

He knows all the plays, keeps score, plans strategy. He's like a baseball freak. He swings in the hammock, listening to ball games and tells me he's restoring balance. Coming into harmony with himself and the world. Looks to me like he's sleeping.

At night, I get into the hammock. I love sleeping beneath the stars. In the city, we might see the moon, occasionally. Out here, there's nothing between me and the night sky. No city's neon glow, no tall trees, no clouds. I lie out looking up, and pretty soon I'm lost in the cosmos.

We got a telescope for Christmas. I've seen incredible things. Planets, nebulas, even the rings of Saturn. Talk about balance. Harmony. It's all a celestial collage. Gazillions of stars scooting around the universe, doing their thing. Every night I see a shooting star. Listen to the coyotes yip and bark. They're out there, circling their prey, hollering at each other across the night. They come right up to the house sometimes. Daytime as well as dark. Everybody's pretty protective of their dogs. We lost our big golden retriever when we first came here. That's when we built the wall around the house.

Yesterday, I took my little brother riding up in the National Forest. That's why we bought here. We're surrounded by National Forest, so we'll never have any neighbors. Dad said he hopes he never sees any people again. He worked in a stock broker's office. Privacy is an unknown word in that world.

My brother Cody is only four, but he loves to go riding. We rode down the wash to the waterfall. Not a real waterfall, but a big rock formation that looks like one. I like to sit on top and look out at the world. Those rocks feel pretty solid, you know. Ruby was grazing and Cody was playing in the wash. It was so still and quiet. The wind was blowing in the tops of the trees, making that whooshing sound. When it's like that, I feel like I'm the only person in the world, and the world is new.

Then all of a sudden, Cody started screaming.

A huge coyote was all over him. He had Cody's arm in his mouth, and was dragging him off. I started screaming and yelling, but the coyote just ignored me. It was like I wasn't even there. So I grabbed some rocks and threw them at him. I hit him a good one, right on his back leg. He dropped Cody's arm and ran off, but not very far. Cody wasn't hurt bad … teeth marks on his arm and claw marks on his face. He was more scared than anything. So was I. I grabbed him up and ran towards Ruby, but that coyote got between us. I didn't know what to do. Cody was crying; the coyote was blocking the way. I turned to get back onto the rocks, but another coyote was behind me. I turned, and there was another, and another. I was surrounded. I've heard how they hunt in packs. And they're not called wily coyote for nothing.

I couldn't get back to Ruby, and I couldn't get back to the rock. I was really scared because those coyotes were out to get me. I could tell by the look in their eyes. They were angry and they were angry at me.

I didn't know what to do. So, I didn't do anything. I just sat down, hugging my little brother, and got perfectly still. Like I wasn't even there. Suddenly, it was like the world just went away, and there was only silence. Total silence. Then, the big male coyote started creeping towards me. I closed my eyes and accepted death.

The big coyote stopped right in front of me. I could see his face so clear. He was smart. That animal was so smart. You could tell by looking at him. So, I asked him, "Are you going to eat me?" Well, he didn't seem to want to eat me, at least not right that minute. So, I asked what he wanted. He looked at me a long time before he spoke. I think he wanted to make sure I'd get it.

He said he was angry as angry can get, and so were all the other coyotes. And the rabbits and deer and pack rats and everybody else. Even the mountain lions, what few there are left. He said this was their home, since forever. Now fences were everywhere. "We no longer walk our ancient trails. Or roam. Or hunt. We're starving, and dying for lack of food and freedom."

So, I asked him, if maybe we couldn't cut a deal. You know … he wouldn't eat me, and I'd promise not to take up any more of his space. He wasn't interested. He just wanted his land back. He and all the rest. 'Cause, more were coming as we sat there. I mean, it was like a coyote convention. Me, surrounded by a circle of wild coyotes. Me and Cody.

I wasn't afraid anymore, and Cody felt safe in my arms. But when I say I wasn't afraid, well, that's not exactly true. I was afraid, but I was so fascinated, I forgot to be afraid. That's probably what saved me. Losing my fear. Cody went to sleep, and so I just sat there, on the ground, communing with the coyotes. It was very bizarre. And very special.

After a while, Charley, that's his name, in human, Charley the chief coyote got up, trotted off and all the others silently followed. No yipping and barking. I watched them disappear behind the ridge. I sat there for a long time, listening to the wind making music with the trees. The world is such a quiet and peaceful place. When you get away from people.

My mom went ballistic. Told me never to go into the canyons again. That's ridiculous. I want to talk to them some more. To Charley. 'Cause, we came here seeking balance. But just being here, we create imbalance. Balance, imbalance. Symmetry, equilibrium. Yin. Yang. Harmony. Those are going to be some pretty wild words to live with.

Change

Tomorrow's the big day. My parents are practically jumping with joy, but I think it's a calamity. I don't see why, just cause my Dad's making good money now, we have to move.

"But we're moving to a better neighborhood," Mom says. Big deal. What's wrong with this one? We've lived here all my life, and it looks pretty good to me.

Mom says everything about the new house is better. It's lots bigger. Yeah. For me to clean on Saturday mornings. A bigger yard. For me to mow. A hot tub. Hello. You think me and my friends will ever get to use it? Forget it. I will have my own room. That'll be good. I like that. My sister's a total brat.

Dad's happy because he won't have to do any repairs on this house. "I've been doing repairs since the day we moved in," he says. Still, why can't they just fix this place up, and maybe make it bigger, so we don't have to move? He says he needs a bigger break on his income tax. I thought people bought houses to live in, not because of taxes.

At least I'm keeping my bedroom furniture. Mom tried to sell it at the garage sale, but I refused. That furniture's going to be my little girl's one day.

Mom says I'm resisting change. She's right. I want everything to stay just like it is. I don't want to have to learn where the glasses go in the new kitchen, or where to put the silverware. Or the towels.

Or meet our new neighbors. They're probably snobby and unfriendly, if they're so much better than we are. If their neighborhood's so much better than ours. Why does everybody always think richer is better?

I am resisting change. It's dumb, I know, because I don't have any choice. Mom says I'll get over it, and love the new house, once we get settled.

All my memories are in this house. I learned to walk around the coffee table. My swing in the big oak out back. Burying the dogs beneath the big magnolia. The banana trees dying every winter and popping back in spring. Those red-headed woodpeckers that wake me up, hammering away on the oak trees out front. The gardenia bushes out by the sidewalk that bloom in May and make everything smell like paradise. Our new house doesn't have any gardenias.

Mom says change is good. Creative. Shakes us out of our rut. Makes us better people. I don't want to be better. I'm fine, just the way I am. Maybe I just don't get it. If change is so good, if moving up in the world is so great, how come it feels like this?

Dear Dad

(Girl sitting, writing.)

Dear Dad. How are you? I hope you're feeling fine.

Get real. How could he possibly be feeling fine? How could anybody?

Dear Dad. How are you? I hope the weather's good.

This is ridiculous. Let's face it. The whole thing is impossible.

Dear Dad. Hello. How's jail treating you? Do they make you wear those orange suits?

Great. Just what every girl wants to brag about. My dad, the convict. Hello. What does your dad do for a living? Oh. Not much. Wears these classy orange jump-suits and picks up trash on the side of the road. What a nightmare.

I don't know what makes me madder. Mom for taking him to court, or Dad for not paying my child support. The judge put him in jail, so I guess I should be mad at him.

Dear Dad. Why didn't you just pay the child support? I'm your only daughter. Couldn't you take care of me just a little? Don't you love me? Oh sure, you said it was really between you and Mom, but I'm the one who did without. So, you see, I guess I don't believe you. 'Cause if you really loved me, it wouldn't matter what happens between you and Mom. You'd still want me to have the best.

Maybe you should live in jail. 'Cause a father's supposed to love his daughter and take care of her and protect her. Be there when she needs him. And I needed you, Dad. Not just your money. You.

Well, you're wearing that crummy orange suit now, and I may just as well get over it. You'd rather spend a year in jail than help me out. That hurts, Dad. That hurts.

It's pretty hard to love you, Dad, after what you did. But, believe it or not, I still do. Maybe jail will do you good. Maybe, by doing without the things that really matter, you'll finally find out what they are. Maybe then you'll be ready to be my dad. Cheers.

The Test

I woke up this morning, jumped out of bed, and got dressed in nothing flat. I was going to be the first person there, if it killed me. I did my makeup and hair extra careful, so I'd look good in my picture. You should see all my friends' driver's licenses. They look like heroin addicts.

I studied my driving pamphlet during breakfast. Mom drove me to the place. I was ready. I knew everything. It was no surprise I aced my written test.

Driving a car is a privilege, not a right, my driving instructor says. Not only is my life in my hands, so are lots of other people. Cars are expensive, and not to be run by the reckless and unready. I know. My cousin was hit by a bad driver last summer and she's had a terrible time. She still walks with a limp.

Getting your driver's license is like becoming an adult. You have to be responsible. A car's a big investment. And I'm paying my own insurance, which ain't cheap.

After the written test, we go outside for the driving test. I got one of those really unfriendly types. Never said a word. Just sat there with his checklist. I was pretty nervous. Not about my ability. About him. He could have at least smiled.

We got in the car, and I did all the right stuff. Seat belt, mirror check, seat adjustment. Turned the key, the engine started, I put it in reverse and stepped on the pedal. We didn't move. I had my foot on the brake. I was so embarrassed, but old sour puss next to me never said a word. He just looked grim.

Finally we got going, and I was doing good. We drove through the obstacle course, and I did all the right things. Turn signals, parallel parked, right turn, left turn, passing, whatever. I was feeling pretty proud of myself, even if what's-his-face next to me was about as gleeful as a mummy.

We got back to the station, to get my picture taken and finish it all off. I was pulling into the parking place when a cat jumped out in front of me. I slammed on the brakes to miss him, which I did. I would have been mortified to kill a cat during my driving test.

Even so, it was bad enough. The car rocked back and forth, and I got real nervous. When I started up again, I accidentally put the car in reverse then hit the gas pedal so hard the car shot out from under me and plowed into the car behind me. I just smacked into it.

My dad's furious. I don't know what this will do to his insurance. Make it go up? And I don't know when I can try again to get my license. I was too depressed to ask.

At least nobody was hurt, and it only dented the guy's back bumper. It's not like it was a major accident. But it was bad enough. I mean, who has a wreck taking their driving test? I'll never hear the end of this at school.

You know the worst? That old grump of an inspector I got stuck with. He laughed. Ha ha ha ha ha. He laughed. Ha ha ha ha ha. Never said a word, never smiled, and when I made a fool out of myself, he laughed. Ha ha ha ha ha ha. I just wish it'd been his car I hit. But it wasn't. Good thing. They'd put me in jail. All I got was a ticket. Reckless driving without a license.

Fire Dancing

(Girl with drum, which she beats from time to time.)

There isn't much to do in our little town. No movie, and the video stores are too pitiful. Mostly, we hang out at each other's place or go hiking and swimming in the woods. Our favorite spot's out at the lake. That's where we build the bonfires. And bonfires are our passion.

Nobody knows how the tradition got started. The best fires are in winter, when it's cold and crisp. Everybody brings their drum, rattle or whatever. We'll drum for hours, watching the fire. I love to catch a spark and ride it up to heaven, lifted by the beat of the drums. Christmas Eve's the biggest fire. Everybody's home from college or the military, or just home for the holidays.

Last Christmas was the best. Everybody was there. The moon was full, the air was clear and bright. It was beautiful. The fire was perfect. Gold and red and blue. And green. And purple.

We got to drumming, and it was wild. Like the drums were alive, and talking to each other in that special language all their own. We drummed about thirty minutes, when out of nowhere this new girl started snaking through the crowd till she got in front of the drummers. She wore a yellow dress that I should look so good in. She had red hair, and looked a bit like the fire herself.

She started dancing. She danced like I've never seen dancing. It wasn't for anybody, like a boyfriend. She was just dancing. For her own self. With her own self.

After a while, another girl joined her and the competition was keen. Then another girl came into the circle, and another. They were dancing like sparks flaming through the night. It was so glorious, so divine, I finally put down my drum and joined them. *(Begins dancing.)* As did almost all the girls. We were all dancing, like nothing existed but the music and the stars, the cold dark air, the hot fire blazing up to heaven. *(Dances.)*

I was in a trance. My body moved and swayed in ways I've never thought before. Like I was learning a new language, one I'd never known before. I was dancing, only someone else was moving. Some other marvelous, magical me that I'd never met, until that night. A me I'm so glad I found, that night, in the drums, and the night and sparks and the fire. *(Dances.)*

Then, one by one, people drifted away. Finally the drummers gave out, too. The only person left standing was the girl in the yellow dress.

I think she came from the fire. And returned to the fire. Because, when I turned my head and looked back again, she was gone. And nobody's seen her since. *(Dances.)*

First Date

Is my hair OK? No. It looks dreadful. I have to do it all over again. I better change this dress too. It's too ... oh, I forgot to paint my toenails. Do I have time? No. He'll be here in ten minutes. He's not already here, is he? That wasn't the doorbell. Is my first date in the whole world ready to begin? No. Thank goodness. Just my brother's dumb video games.

Why do I have to look so awful for my first date? I thought I'd be a radiant beauty. But here I am looking like The Terror. What if he doesn't come? What if he stands me up, on my very first date? He wouldn't. He's not like that. Then why isn't he here yet? Because it isn't 7:30, stupid. Besides, he'd call if he was going to be late. He's that kind of guy. Isn't he?

I don't even know him, actually. Why am I going out with him? Have I lost my mind? Am I crazy? He might be a serial killer, or a mad sex fiend. What are we going to talk about? What do you talk about on a date? What if he talks about sex? I could talk about the math test. Nobody wants to hear about a math test on a date. They want to hear romantic things.

I don't know any romantic things. What if he tries to kiss me? Horrors. What if he doesn't? What if he doesn't like me? What if I don't like him? How did I get myself into this? Oh, I'm going to be sick. Breathe, Abigail, breathe. *(Takes deep breath).* Breathe. *(Takes several breaths.)*

Why did I say I'd go out with him? He's so weird-looking. And acts so strange in class. I never thought I'd go out with anybody like him. I mean, he is kind of cute, in his own way, but ... what if, oh no! What if he can't find my house? I did give him directions, didn't I? Does he have my phone number in case he gets lost?

I'm all worn out now. I'm exhausted. I better call him and cancel. Tell him I can't go because I'm too tired. I can't do that. He'll think I'm a lunatic. This is awful. We're going to have a terrible time. Just terrible. Breathe, Abigail. *(Takes deep breath.)* Breathe. *(Takes several deep breaths.)* There. It's going to be fine. We're going to have a great time and it will be lovely.

Oh no! The doorbell. It's only 7:30. He's supposed to be late. Why is he on time? What am I going to do? You go answer the door, let him in, and say hello. Then you go out on your first date. Oh no. I can't. I' m too scared. Breathe, Abigail. Breathe. *(Takes several deep breaths.)*

Now. Hair, nails, lipstick. I look great. Oh, this is too much fun. We're going to have such a great time. *(Opens door.)* Hi, Roger. Gee, you look great.

Swamp Fire

The swamp is a forbidden place, fit only for beasts. It's a hidden world of green and speckled things. Slithering things. Sliding, gliding, drifting things.

My mama used to tell me stories of the dreaded Fifolet, the evil Swamp Monster who gobbles up everyone who wanders into his wicked world. She said that swamp fire is his head, which he holds in his hands and throws high in the air to scare little girls, like me. My daddy'd make hideous Fifolet sounds, scaring me to death. He said the Fifolet's roar silences the alligators. And he stinks so bad, even the skunks go running. The Fifolet eats everything, but especially loves little girls, they are so sweet and soft and juicy. Just like you.

Have you ever seen swamp fire? It burns in the distance, a ghostly light fueled by a world feeding on itself. Death and decay turned into glowing pinks, reds, greens, blues. Rot into strange and flickering, glowing balls of light bouncing off the land like arctic lights cascading down from the stars. Swamp fire, fox fire, always hovers unreachable, just beyond the horizon. It's hiding just behind the trees. Darting beneath a shadow. Leaping into view only to flee.

The swamp is an endless cycle of death and rebirth. It's constantly renewing itself and I think that swamp fire is its haunted soul slipping ever between the worlds searching for its home.

I love the swamp. I love the feel of it, the smell of it, the way it wraps itself around me, holding me spellbound by all the sounds and sights. There's a little green frog who lounges invisible on a clump of water lilies, a red line across its tiny cheek. Or a snapping turtle napping hidden in plain sight on a speckled log. Blue herons stand among the reeds, still like death. Alligators, jaws open wide, wait. Black bears roar somewhere, over there. Panthers hide in the foliage high on a sturdy limb until they become black death leaping on its prey.

The swamp is silent. Still. Streams run so hushed one feels the rushing water. I'm always peaceful in the swamp. Being alone in its vast expanse is like being the only person on earth.

Since my parents died in that plane crash a year ago all I want is to be away from everybody and everything. I feel so unloved, and so unloving. And unlovable. Besides, people want too much from me, things I don't have to give. Things like a smile, a nod, a hello. Animals expect nothing, want nothing, except the bugs drinking my blood for breakfast. It's all right. They can have it.

The other day, I was out fishing. My pirogue slid silent through the tiny green duck weed floating on the bayou. I drifted beneath the cypress trees, touching their bony knees sticking up above the water, thinking how I'd like to paint them into fantastical creatures, maybe even Father Christmas and the Magi. But I probably never will.

I drifted in a small circle, going nowhere. My fingers dragged the water. It was cool like autumn wind. A water moccasin swam by, but didn't bother me. The fish were jumping in and out of the stream, casting little pools of ripples on the water. Mullets and croakers darted through the air snatching up bugs.

I looked down into the water. My self looked back. I saw my hair braided and tasseled down my back. My skin's burned dark from so much time outside. A stranger might think I was just another swamp creature, doing my thing.

Just then, a fish no bigger than my hand hurdled straight up at me. Its mouth brushed against my face, leaving a damp spot on my cheek and lips. I touched the wet place on my face and, for the first time in weeks, maybe even months, I smiled. I actually smiled. Then I laughed. I laughed and laughed and laughed, like I was crazy. That little fish had leapt straight up out of the water and kissed me.

Goddess of War and Wisdom

When I was thirteen, I discovered Napoleon. Then Alexander, then Hannibal. All the great warriors. Genghis Khan. Atilla. I was totally fascinated.

When I was 15, my sister dated a guy from West Point. He lent me his books on military strategy. Light summer reading, y'know?

Look. I know it sounds weird. Maybe it is. Everybody's out swimming and working on their tan, and I'm curled up with Robert E. Lee at Gettysburg. What can I say? It's my thing. I'd recreate the battles on paper and in my mind, and every time, I'd outsmart all those guys. Yes. Even Patton.

Ever read *The Odyssey*? About the Trojan War? I have. Twice. That's when I discovered the Goddess of War. Athena was Goddess of Wisdom too, but she was the greatest military strategist of them all. Better even than Aries, who was really a wuss.

That's when I stopped worrying about it. If Athena was good enough for the Greeks, she was good enough for me. I found Cleopatra too. She was just like Athena. Very wise, to be so young, and defended her country with the best of them. Too bad Marc Antony lost it for her, but that's another story.

Two weeks from today, I'll be joining the military corps of cadets at West Point. I'll be there four years, and within twenty, I'll be a General.

My mom thinks I'm crazy. She wants me to become a nurse, marry a doctor and have a happy life. I will have a happy life. No better place than West Point to meet handsome, healthy guys. I just want to marry one who also wants a military career.

None of this is because I think war's so great. I don't. It's probably the most horrible thing anybody's ever thought up. I never met a woman who liked war.

It's because I hate war so much, that I want to be in the military. All those guys with war genes, who love to fight, and think war the most glorious event of a lifetime? Who think killing's planting the flag on top of macho mountain? The only reason wars drag on for years and years is 'cause guys love fighting so much they'll do anything to keep it going. From a barroom brawl to Bosnia. Gives their lives meaning.

No. People like me should be running the military. People like me, women, who hate it, and want to end it. I know I'm smarter than those guys, and stopping them is the best way I can think of to use my brains.

Nowheresville

Who wants to spend six weeks in nowheresville? Thirty miles from a loaf of bread. Fifty from a movie. Forget TV. This place is like outer space.

With your aunt, who nobody in the family ever talks about without prefacing her name with weird. Weird Aunt Sassafras. I mean, her name's weird enough isn't it? Sassafras. Nobody's named Sassafras. Well, my weird aunt is. I guess she could have chosen an even weirder name. I heard of one artist who named herself Magenta. Muriel Magenta. We know what color she liked.

I told my folks, when they decided to spend the summer in Europe, without me ... they were trying to save their marriage, but didn't want me to know. What's not to know? I told them I could take very good care of myself, thank you, and no way was I going off to Montana to live on the top of a mountain with my weird aunt. Odd, isn't it, how after years of hardly speaking to Aunt Sassafras, my mother suddenly decides I should get to know her?

Well, I went prepared. CD player, suitcase full of junk food, another full of videos. She has a TV and video player, for watching art films.

She met me at the airport. She didn't look very weird. Actually, she's very pretty. Long brown hair braided down her back. Pretty blue eyes with long black lashes. Great figure. Better than Mom. Soft spoken, rather jolly. I liked her right off. And she liked me.

Driving to her house, which is some house. It's made out of rocks. Big, beautiful, enormous rocks. Like it's a big rock itself, coming out of the earth. I've never seen anything like it. There isn't anything like it. Everything's solar too. At least in summer. She even has a solar oven where the sun does all the cooking. Best food I ever ate.

Anyway, driving to her house, guess what we see? I couldn't believe it. A herd of buffalo, a herd of elk, three moose — that might be meese, but I'm never sure — about a trillion hawks and a bald eagle. I'm not kidding. All those animals I've seen pictures of all my life, I'm meeting them, in the flesh. I wanted to get out and talk to the buffalo, but Sassafras wouldn't let me. Said they were dangerous wild beasts. They didn't look so dangerous, sitting along the side of the road taking a nap.

That night, just at dusk, as we were sitting out on the deck watching the sunset, a bear came tromping through the woods. A big, really big grizzly bear. I was so scared. I saw *The Edge.* And she told me, never leave any food out. In fact, she has a steel-lined locked pantry, to keep all the critters out.

And a big fireplace, which we lit every night. It gets cold up there when the sun goes down. It isn't that warm during the day either. I loved wearing sweaters in summer.

She let me go into her studio with her every morning. She does everything ... paints, makes jewelry, works in clay making these incredibly fantastical sculptures of gargoyles and angels and all manner of demons and dragons. Her house is a wonderland of bright colors and beautiful paintings and art everywhere. Even her sink's a painting. I've never seen anything like it, but I want one.

I painted too. Did pretty good considering I've never had any art before. I'd sit outside and paint whatever I saw. She said I was pretty good. She showed me a few tricks, like mixing colors, but mostly she let me blunder my way though. I'd tell her I messed up, and she said to keep going. So, I did.

I'm going back next summer. In fact, I'll probably go to college up there. I might major in art, although Dad says that's a dumb idea 'cause I'll starve to death and end up like my weird aunt. Looks to me like she's got a pretty nice life.

Oh. Those art films she says she watches. Guess what? *(Whispers.)* Sassafras is a closet Bruce Lee fan. She's got every movie he ever made. She also likes westerns, and has a whole collection of cowboy movies. Now, that's pretty weird, don't you think?

Mom or Me

She's late again. Probably won't even come home. I never know what she's gonna do. I just don't want her bringing her dates home for the night. Makes me feel creepy.

I guess if I'd been married since forever and now had a chance to party, I'd do it too. But every night practically? While I'm stuck home with my brother and sister. Studying. I'd like to go out myself, every once in a while.

I'd like to see my parents too. But Mom's gone at least half the time, and even though I'm supposed to see Dad on weekends, he's always off with his latest girlfriend. I didn't know when your folks got a divorce, you practically end up an orphan.

Almost seems like I'm the mom and she's the teenager. She's having all the fun. I thought these were supposed to be the best years of my life. What ... study, study, study, so I won't end up like her? Divorced and working in a dead end job.

I'd like to date. Not that I fault her. I don't. She's entitled. Dad's dating every woman he sees, so I hear. He even dated one of my classmate's mom. I hope he doesn't marry her. I couldn't stand having Rowena for a stepsister. Gag.

At least I'll be going away to college in another year. Dad's springing for it, and I know I'll get a scholarship. With all the studying I do, and my grades. When I get to college, forget books. All I'm going to do is party, party, party. And I'm never having kids. I've served three years of early motherhood already — I've had it.

Sure, I'm jealous. I know it. Can't help it. When they got the divorce, I wanted to go with Dad. I knew I'd end up her slave, always having to look out for the kids. And that's what's happened.

It isn't fair. It just isn't fair. I should be the one dating and partying, not her. I mean, who's the teenager here? Mom or me?

I can't wait to get out of here. I can't wait.

Just a Date

It's not right. It just isn't right. How could it happen? I don't know. I don't know. I know it's not my fault. I know that. But still.

It was just a date.

It's not like we were in love. We were friends. He was my sister's friend, really. Always hanging around the house with that gang of hers. Then, when they all went off to college last month, I never even thought about him. I was totally surprised when he called and asked me out. I figured he was homesick and needed a friend. It was just a date. A simple Friday night date. A movie, a pizza. Nothing exciting or romantic. A simple date with a friend.

I've heard about those fraternity parties. Somebody told me the object of the party is to get as drunk as you can as fast as you can. He wasn't like that in high school. Not with his folks. They're pretty old, you know. He was born like, late in life. Their only child.

A date. One little date.

When he called from the party, to tell me he was late, but that he'd be here, I told him not to come. I could tell he'd been drinking. I told him we could go out tomorrow, or next weekend or whenever. I said that the road was too dangerous, with all that new construction. There's at least a foot drop off from the concrete. Besides, it was pouring down rain. I told him not to come. Don't come, I said. Don't come. Please don't come.

I can't go to the funeral. How can I face his parents? They must hate me. Everybody must hate me. I even hate me.

Everybody says it's not my fault, and I guess I know that. But still. If I'd never told him I'd go out with him in the first place, this never would have happened. I mean, it wasn't any big deal. It was a date. It was just a date. That's all. A dumb, stupid date. How did it ever turn into this?

Erased

I got an A today. In real class. I never got an A before. Not in real class. Not even in Special Ed. We get reports in Special Ed. They don't give us grades. I got a B once. In real class. In House. School calls it Home Ec, but we call it House. I cut up all the carrots, with the big knife, and got all the carrots in the soup pot and never spilled a single one. And the onions, and the green beans. Not even any. And I didn't cut myself.

My Nana was so cheery when I got a B, she made me a big chocolate cake, just like my birthday. But it wasn't my birthday. My birthday's in August and we always go swimming. She put a gold star on my cake.

I study real hard. But, some things ... I just don't know. Like how to make the numbers go righty. They always go somewhere but not where they're s'posed to. Running all over the page and jumping up and down. They so bad. Letters too. 'N words. Putting themselves together so nobody can tell they story. I erase all the bad numbers and words. I get big holes in my page. I give up tryin' to make 'em go righty. My new teacher, in Special Ed, don't get all mad at me. When I mess up and erase and get holes in my paper. My old teacher did. She said I had more holes in my head than in my paper. Know what I think? I think she got erased. But I didn't tell nobody what she done to me. Not nobody. Not ever. Not even my Nana.

We make hamburgers in House. Sometimes I get to cook. When we play cafe. 'Sometimes I gets to be the folks who eat. That's the best part. 'Specially the french fries.

We make hamburgers on my birthday too. Mama used to make

'em. Now Nana and Poppy cook. But they don't taste the same. Nana says they justly the same, but they not. Nana makes the best hamburgers in the whole world.

Mama was like my old teacher. Sometimes. She said I had holes in my head too. She was wrong. I looked in the mirror and never saw a single one.

An' I never told nobody what she done to me. I never, never, never told nobody. I promise. Not nobody. Not ever. I don't know why she got erased. But she did. I ask Nana if she's coming back but she just wobbles her head and says, "That girl. That girl. Where did I go wrong?"

I don't think Nana's wrong. She knows everything. How to make the numbers go righty. She reads whole books to me at night, and gets all the words right. She tucks me in my bed and kisses me when the sandman comes to put sleep in my eyes. Nana says for me to have sweet sugar dreams. Or ice cream dreams. Or apple pie dreams.

My Nana's gonna be real cheery about my A. I take Chorus, in real school. We sing lots. I sang a song all the way through, all by myself without the teacher helping me at all. You want to hear my song?

Row, row, row your boat
Gently down the stream.
Merrily, merrily, merrily, merrily
Life is but a dream.

Sometimes I dream about Mama. But not so much now. Mostly I dream about my teacher. She so pretty. So happy. She sweet, like chocolate candy. I love her. I think maybe she's my new mama.

(Exits singing.)

Merrily, merrily, merrily, merrily
Life is but a dream.

Duets

A Room All by Myself

ANNIE: Well, tomorrow's the big day. How does it feel? Going away to college.

MITZI: Kinda scary. I think I'm supposed to feel all grown up, but I really don't. Don't get me wrong. I am excited.

ANNIE: I'm going to miss you.

MITZI: I'll miss you, too.

ANNIE: No you won't. You'll be so busy going to classes, meeting guys, going to parties, you won't even think about me.

MITZI: You think I'll meet lots of guys?

ANNIE: With your looks, they'll be climbing the dorm walls, trying to get in.

MITZI: It'll be kind of nice, starting a new life. Leaving high school behind, moving into adulthood.

ANNIE: Does going to college make you an adult?

MITZI: So, you going to take care of Mom and Dad for me?

ANNIE: Don't you have it backwards?

MITZI: Dad won't have anybody to go jogging with, and now Mom'll have to try to teach you to cook.

ANNIE: Something you successfully avoided for eighteen years.

MITZI: Just think, you'll finally get what you always wanted.

ANNIE: What? A room all by myself?

MITZI: You'll be the only one here. You'll have their undivided attention.

ANNIE: That may not be such a good thing, you know.

MITZI: Enjoy it while it lasts, 'cause next year, you're out of here too.

ANNIE: I'm not going to college.

MITZI: Since when?

ANNIE: Since I saw all the hoops you had to jump through to get in. And the stress on Mom and Dad, wondering how to pay for all this.

MITZI: Oh, they've got plenty of money.

ANNIE: They just want us to think they do. I've heard them talking late into the night, figuring out how to do things.

MITZI: Like what? That new car I didn't get.

ANNIE: Like, all those new clothes. And books. And that computer.

MITZI: What, a used laptop? That couldn't have cost very much.

ANNIE: Just try to make it last, OK?

MITZI: Let's not quarrel, on my last night. Tell me....

ANNIE: What?

MITZI: Oh, you'll think I'm being silly.

ANNIE: You are silly.

MITZI: Oh, Annie. Who's going to keep me honest, if you're not around?

ANNIE: So. You've got everything packed, right?

MITZI: Right.

ANNIE: Even the teddy bear Aunt Shelly made, when you were six.

MITZI: Whither I goest, she goest.

ANNIE: So, I guess that's it then. We can go to bed.

MITZI: Just think. This is the last night I'll be sleeping here.

ANNIE: Mitzi, you're only going to college, not Outer Mongolia. You'll be home for Thanksgiving.

MITZI: I guess. Annie ...

ANNIE: What?

MITZI: Oh, nothing.

ANNIE: What?

MITZI: Promise you won't think I'm dumb.

ANNIE: You are dumb.

MITZI: I know, but ...

ANNIE: I know. If you get homesick, I'll accept your collect calls.

MITZI: Thanks.

ANNIE: And if you don't get a date for homecoming, I'll dress up like Brad Pitt and come be your escort.

MITZI: *(Laughs.)*

ANNIE: And if you flunk out, I'll cover for you. I'll tell the folks you went on a student exchange program to France. They'll be impressed.

MITZI: *(Laughs.)* Oh, Annie. You should be going to school, not me. You got all the family smarts.

ANNIE: Yeah, well. It's getting late. Let's call it quits.

MITZI: OK. Oh, and Annie ...

ANNIE: Uh-huh.

MITZI: I love you.

ANNIE: Uh-huh.

MITZI: And I really will miss you.

ANNIE: Uh-huh.

MITZI: Night.

ANNIE: Night. *(Pause)* I love you too, Mitzi. You're gonna do great, Mitzi, you're gonna do just great.

MITZI: I sure hope so. Night.

Sally and Mary

SALLY: You ready?
MARY: Uh ...
SALLY: Don't tell me you forgot.
MARY: Uh ...
SALLY: The museum. The Egyptians ... Isis, Cleopatra, Ra, all that good stuff ... hieroglyphics, pyramids ... mummies ...
MARY: Uh ...
SALLY: No. You didn't. You couldn't.
MARY: Well ...
SALLY: You promised. You made a commitment. I bought the tickets. They're only good for today. It's the big opening.
MARY: Jenny would love to go.
SALLY: We never get to go anyplace together. Either I'm working or you're working. Or you have a date, or I do.
MARY: I'm sorry.
SALLY: No you aren't.
MARY: You're right. I'm not.
SALLY: So stop being a hypocrite.
MARY: OK. I'm not sorry.
SALLY: So where are you going?
MARY: Oh, you know.
SALLY: No, I don't know. Oh. You're not. You can't.
MARY: I can and I am.
SALLY: Now my feelings really are hurt. How could you do this to me?
MARY: I'm not doing it to you. I'm doing it for me. Can I wear your brown cashmere sweater?
SALLY: You don't ask for much, do you?

MARY: And I need some money.
SALLY: What are you gonna do next? Ask for the moon?
MARY: How much do you have?
SALLY: I spent all my money on tickets to see Cleopatra.
MARY: Your new silk scarf?
SALLY: I haven't even worn it yet.
MARY: I have to look my best.
SALLY: You could put a paper bag on your head and look good. He doesn't care what you wear. He probably doesn't even know what you look like.
MARY: So. Can I borrow it?
SALLY: Sure. Anything else?
MARY: Your pearls?
SALLY: No. Not the pearls.
MARY: Please?
SALLY: No. Don't ask again.
MARY: OK, OK. You don't have to get excited.
SALLY: I am excited. I'm mad and I'm hurt. I don't like to be treated this way.
MARY: I'll make it up to you. We'll go to the ...
SALLY: The what? The movies? Big deal. Watch some stupid car chase. Who cares?
MARY: OK. We'll do something else. Whatever you want.
SALLY: You don't see him for a zillion years and as soon as he shows up, you drop everything.
MARY: I can't live in the past. If we're to have any future together, I have to do this.
SALLY: Well, good luck. Where's your coat?
MARY: I left it at work.
SALLY: Take mine.
MARY: It isn't very cold.
SALLY: Take it. It's colder than you think. Where are you going, anyway?
MARY: I don't know. I don't think he has much money, so we'll probably just walk around somewhere. Sit on a park bench. I don't know.
SALLY: Here. Take the tickets.

MARY: Oh no. I couldn't.

SALLY: Yes you can.

MARY: Are you sure?

SALLY: I'm sure. Take 'em. And have a good time. What are you going to talk to him about anyway?

MARY: I don't know.

SALLY: Why are you doing this?

MARY: Because, if I don't get my relationship with him cleared up, I'll never be able to have any kind of relationship with any other man.

SALLY: I never want to see him again. Ever.

MARY: Maybe one day you will.

SALLY: I doubt it. Here. Take the tickets. Give you something to do. Something to talk about how Cleopatra rolled herself up in a carpet to go see Julius Caesar.

MARY: And how she died by the bite of an asp.

SALLY: Can you imagine that? Sticking your hand in a basket knowing a poisonous snake's going to bite you?

MARY: I guess she did what she had to do.

SALLY: Here. Take the tickets. Go on. Take them. I insist. I command you. Take these tickets, go to the museum and have a great time.

MARY: Thanks.

SALLY: And tell him I think he's a no-good loser and if he ever comes to see me, I'll punch him out, OK?

MARY: OK.

SALLY: Tell him I hope he falls into a crocodile pit and a cave full of rattlesnakes and vipers. OK?

MARY: OK.

SALLY: Tell him I pray nightly that the fleas of a thousand camels nest in his armpits. OK?

MARY: OK.

SALLY: Now, go, and have a good time.

MARY: Sure you don't want to come? He asked us both.

SALLY: No. I don't want to go.

MARY: I bet you do.

SALLY: No. I don't. I never want to see him again. When he called last week, I couldn't believe it. After all these years, he wants to see us. After he walked out of our lives without any notice. Why would I want to see him?

MARY: Because he's our father.

SALLY: We have a real father now. Who loves us, provides for us, takes us places. To the doctor, the dentist. Remembers our birthdays. Helps with our schoolwork. No, Mary. You go. You go work out your relationship with a man who deserted you, abandoned you, and never spent a dime to support you. I'll stay right here. And don't condemn me for doing what I think is right.

MARY: Will you do the same for me?

SALLY: Here. You want these pearls?

MARY: Thanks. But ...

SALLY: It's OK. Really. Wear 'em if you want.

MARY: No. Thanks anyway. Want to go skating tomorrow?

SALLY: Maybe.

MARY: I'll see you later, OK?

SALLY: OK.

MARY: Sure you don't want to come?

SALLY: I'm sure. I'm very, very sure.

MARY: OK. Bye.

SALLY: Bye. Oh, and Mary? Don't stick your hands in any stray baskets you see floating around.

MARY: If you'll promise not to go rolling yourself up in any carpets.

SALLY: Bye.

MARY: Bye.

Juliet, Revisited

ROSANNA: You're auditioning for her? Why on earth would anyone ever want to play Juliet?

MARIAH: Because. She's beautiful. She's adored. Loved. Worshiped.

ROSANNA: She's dead.

MARIAH: But she died for love.

ROSANNA: Give me a break. Nobody dies for love. She had a martyr complex. Or a death wish.

MARIAH: But Romeo killed himself because he couldn't live without her.

ROSANNA: Men are like that. They can't cope.

MARIAH: You are so cynical.

ROSANNA: I am realistic. Look, if you audition for the part ...

MARIAH: I'm going to audition and win. You'll see.

ROSANNA: You'll be setting a terrible example for future generations.

MARIAH: Just because you aren't up to all that acting ability ...

ROSANNA: I wouldn't play Juliet if she was the only character in the world. I'd rather play Bugs Bunny than Juliet. You just don't get it.

MARIAH: Get what?

ROSANNA: Killing yourself over some guy. Thinking you can't live without him. Throwing yourself on the grave and downing a vial of poison. Offing yourself with a dagger. That's rot. Really. Juliet is not a very positive role model.

MARIAH: Gee. You feel pretty strongly about this, don't you?

ROSANNA: Oh, go on and be Juliet. It's only a stage play. It's no big deal.

MARIAH: No. Maybe you're right. Maybe I should try out for another part. I know. I'll be the nurse. She's pretty earthy. That'll be fun.

ROSANNA: Hey. Hands off. That's my part. I'm auditioning to play her.

MARIAH: Since you talked me out of being Juliet, what's left? Except for the mother, and she's kind of out of it, don't you think?

ROSANNA: Did you know that in Shakespeare's time women weren't allowed to be actors?

MARIAH: Uh-unh.

ROSANNA: It's true. Juliet was played by a thirteen-year-old boy, before his voice changed.

MARIAH: No way.

ROSANNA: Really.

MARIAH: I don't think I even want to be in this play, do you?

ROSANNA: Yeah. I do.

MARIAH: So. Now we're both trying for the same role. So that's it. May the best actor win.

ROSANNA: What a thrill. Break a leg.

Jeopardy

ELLAZINE: Are you going out with him tonight, Jamie?
JAMIE: Who are you?
ELLAZINE: His real girlfriend, Jamie.
JAMIE: Who are you talking about?
ELLAZINE: You know who, Jamie.
JAMIE: OK. I get it. We're playing Jeopardy. I have to know the answer before I get the question.
ELLAZINE: Are you going out with him tonight?
JAMIE: Oh. Ellazine. I know who you are. I've heard about you.
ELLAZINE: Then you know I mean what I say.
JAMIE: Right. You're the Mafia, huh. What are you going to do? Beat me up? Punch me out? Throw me in the river with weights on my feet, Ellazine?
ELLAZINE: I might.
JAMIE: Get real.
ELLAZINE: When? Where?
JAMIE: Is this a threat, Ellazine?
ELLAZINE: A challenge. There's nothing I'd like better than to take care of you.
JAMIE: Oh yeah. Well, choose your weapon. Fists. Knives. Guns. Uzis. That's the weapon of choice for terrorists, isn't it? What's with you anyway, terrorizing me because some guy talked to me in the hall?
ELLAZINE: I saw how he leaned over to talk to you.
JAMIE: Nice, wasn't it? He's the perfect height.
ELLAZINE: And how he looked at you.
JAMIE: Very romantic, wasn't it?

ELLAZINE: And how you looked at him.

JAMIE: He seemed to like it.

ELLAZINE: I didn't.

JAMIE: I loved it. I thought it was great.

ELLAZINE: It better not happen again.

JAMIE: I plan to talk to him again tomorrow, believe it or not, Ellazine.

ELLAZINE: You don't want to do that, Jamie.

JAMIE: I don't really care. You don't decide who I talk to and who I don't. And I'm through talking to you, Ellazine.

ELLAZINE: Don't you walk away from me.

JAMIE: Ciao. *(Exits.)*

ELLAZINE: Jamie. Come back. Jamie. I'll get you, girl. Just wait. I'll get you.

Lord Zandriel and the Metatrons

(B.T. is engaged in some activity – reading, painting, dancing, yoga. Gwen enters, excited.)

GWEN: You are never going to guess what's happening. It's the greatest thing I've ever heard.

BT: Uh huh.

GWEN: You're going to love it.

BT: Uh huh.

GWEN: Would you please talk to me?

BT: Uh huh.

GWEN: BT.

BT: OK. *(Continues doing her thing.)*

GWEN: Hello. Earth to BT.

BT: What? What do you want?

GWEN: You are never going to guess what's happening. Today!

BT: It's your birthday?

GWEN: No. Listen. This is the greatest. Really. You know how we've been doing that Save the Earth thing for Earth Day. Listen. We don't have to do it anymore.

BT: What, they cancelled Earth?

GWEN: Listen. There's this guy. He's out in Hawaii right now. Today. As we speak.

BT: Gwendolyn. Take a deep breath.

GWEN: It's all over the internet. Lord Zandriel of the planet Metatron is landing today. In Hawaii.

BT: Great. Tell him hello.

GWEN: No, no. You don't understand. The Galactic Federation has launched this project ... Intervention Earth. Lord Uriel and

Lord Ariel are leading the troops.

BT: And they're landing in Hawaii. Good. They can work on their tan.

GWEN: No, no. They're coming to save us. To save the planet.

BT: That's downright thoughtful of 'em.

GWEN: Actually, we're going to save the planet. See, when they land, we ...

BT: Us earthlings? Save our own planet. Uh huh.

GWEN: We're all going to ascend to full consciousness. We'll all be so wonderful, we won't go around polluting anymore, or doing bad things. There'll be no more crime. Or war. Everything will be perfect.

BT: Great. We could all use some higher consciousness.

GWEN: This guy, I forgot his name, but he's been going back and forth to the planet Metatron since he was a kid. He's got these probes all in his back.

BT: Oh. Probes. In his back. Like Frankenstein. Sticking out of his neck.

GWEN: The Metatrons put them there so they can tell him what's happening. On the galactic plane.

BT: Sounds like he's got a few probes in his brain, too.

GWEN: BT, this is serious.

BT: It's gotta be, if Lord Uriel and Lord Ariel are involved. C'mon Gwendolyn, get real. Lord Zandriel. Of the planet Metropolis. This sounds like bad science fiction.

GWEN: The planet Metatron. People all over the planet know about this. They have meetings, and are planning what to do when we all ascend to full consciousness.

BT: I'm all in favor of higher consciousness, but this is a joke.

GWEN: It is not. The probe guy's in Hawaii, right now. He's the welcoming committee.

BT: He's gonna feel pretty stupid standing in the ocean all day, and nobody comes. Oh well, he can work on his tan. Forget him. After today, he'll be so embarrassed he'll probably teleport himself off to, what's the planet ... Metronome?

GWEN: Metatron. It's in the Sirius galaxy. All the spaceships are going to shift into the fifth dimension at a point near planet

Maldek, via the inter-dimensional bubble within the Photon Belt.

BT: Right. And when they don't make it through the photons, you'll never hear from him again. Web site deleted. Lost in cyberspace.

GWEN: Look, you know how bad things are. It's all so complicated. So big.

BT: What? Those few minor problems like save the rain forest, patch up the ozone, global warming, new diseases, toxic dumping, polluted water, vanishing species ... those picky little things?

GWEN: Nobody cares.

BT: Nobody knows what to do. Where do you start? How do you organize the whole planet to save itself, before it's too late. Before the earth just gives up and quits.

GWEN: Maybe it's already too late.

BT: It's like Easter Island.

GWEN: That's the place with the statues, right?

BT: That's all there is. Huge statues of faces, with funny hats on their heads. Well, some of them have hats.

GWEN: Why just some of them?

BT: Maybe they were the good guys. Nobody knows. Maybe they were the bad.

GWEN: What does that have to do with this?

BT: The Easter Islanders destroyed their island. They cut down all the trees, probably to roll those statues down the mountain. Their world was dying and so were they. So they started worshiping this Bird god, who was gonna fly down and carry them off to a better world, paradise. All they did those last few years, as they slowly starved to death, was sit around and wait for the Bird god.

GWEN: So, what happened?

BT: He was a no-show. They all died.

GWEN: Oh.

BT: That's what your probe guy's talking about. And why people want to believe him. Because it's easy. We have made a mess. Since nobody knows what to do, why not Lord Zandriel, the

Bird god, swooping down from Metrapol. Let him do it, 'cause us poor pitiful earthlings can't.

GWEN: Maybe we can't.

BT: We created pyramids and atomic bombs and lasers. MTV and diet coke. Restaurants that spin around on the top of buildings. We've been to the moon, for heaven's sake. Put an erector set on Mars.

GWEN: But I want them to land.

BT: You and me, we're going to be part of the big world someday. I think we can make a difference. Maybe you don't, but I do. And I want to. I don't want Megatrons or Martians or whatever coming down to rescue us. We can save ourselves. But if we all sit around waiting for Lord Zandriel, we won't do anything. I hope they never come.

GWEN: But what if they don't? And we don't? Or we can't.

BT: All that'll be left is a bunch of carved rocks wearing stupid hats. And it won't matter who the good guys are, or the bad. Higher consciousness or not, I don't want probes sticking out of this body. Or this brain. Earthlings may not be perfect, but a lot of people are out there trying. It may take us a while, but I think we can do it.

GWEN: Well, when Lord Zandriel and the Galactic Fleet land, you tell them that.

BT: The only things landing on the beach in Hawaii today are surfers.

GWEN: I don't know. I just think it would be nice if we did ascend to a higher level of consciousness. If we all became better people.

BT: Gwendolyn, you're the bestest people I know.

GWEN: So are you. Oh.

BT: Oh?

GWEN: Oh.

TOGETHER: Oh. Yo.

Who's Mad?

DEVINA: So where were you last night?

KATE: What are you so mad about?

DEVINA: So, where were you?

KATE: Home, studying for Mrs. Wilson's test. As if it's any of your business.

DEVINA: You're such a liar. I can't stand people who lie.

KATE: Excuse me?

DEVINA: You were out with Angela's boyfriend, weren't you?

KATE: Excuse me?

DEVINA: You and Roger were parked out by the lake. And the last time I looked, like yesterday afternoon, Roger and Angela were going steady.

KATE: Last time I looked, it wasn't anybody's business but mine where I was last night.

DEVINA: Where are you going?

KATE: To hire a lawyer, since you're the new police, District Attorney, judge and jury who's convicted me for a crime that never happened.

DEVINA: I saw you.

KATE: I don't know what or who you think you saw, but I have to get to class.

DEVINA: You can't walk away from me like that.

KATE: Oh. OK. I'll walk like this.

DEVINA: *(Grabs her by the arm and holds her.)* You were out with Roger last night, and the night before that and the night before that. I saw you. I know what you did. Now you have to tell the truth about it. You have to go to Angela and apologize. You have to promise never to do it again.

KATE: You're crazy. Get away from me. Don't you ever come near me again.

DEVINA: I'm not going to let you get away with it. It's wrong. You can't do that to her.

KATE: Devina, don't you think you're a little over the top here? I mean, why are you so mad about something that doesn't even concern you?

DEVINA: I'm not mad.

KATE: You're about to punch me out. Over something that isn't even your business. I'd say you're not only mad, you're irrational.

DEVINA: I never get mad.

KATE: Tell that to the tooth fairy.

DEVINA: I don't. I never get mad. It isn't ladylike.

KATE: Ladylike. Is that like the Olympics? Ladies' figure skating. Ladies' slalom. Ladies' mogul. Isn't that an oxymoron?

DEVINA: I am not a moron.

KATE: Oh.

DEVINA: I won't get mad because you insulted me. Anger is a negative emotion.

KATE: Oh, but you do it so well.

DEVINA: I do not.

KATE: You're a master at it, Devina. A world class mad meister.

DEVINA: You can't change the subject away from you and Roger.

KATE: Me and Roger is a non-event. I don't know what you're doing prowling the streets at night like some avenging angel looking for sinners, but I'm not one of them.

DEVINA: Well, who was he with then?

KATE: I couldn't care less. And neither should you.

DEVINA: But I do care.

KATE: Why?

DEVINA: Because, it's wrong. To cheat on somebody. It's wrong.

KATE: So. It's wrong. Big deal.

DEVINA: Don't you care?

KATE: No.

DEVINA: *(Slaps her.)* It's people like you that make everything so horrible. You don't care about anything or anybody. Just yourself. Get out of here. I hate you, and everybody like you.

KATE: You're not being unladylike, are you?

DEVINA: What?

KATE: Unladylike. You know. Hostile, aggressive, and in other words, angry. You know. Mad. M-A-D. As in rabid. Foaming at the mouth, furious ...

DEVINA: *(Goes after her with a vengeance. KATE skips around the stage, parrying her thrusts, until DEVINA, frustrated and angry, begins to cry. KATE exits as DEVINA throws herself on the floor screaming and sobbing as huge waves of anger pour out of her.)*

He Promised, Never Again

CARMEN: What happened to you?

ANGELA: *(Covers black eye.)* Ran into a door.

CARMEN: I thought you dumped him after he hit you last time.

ANGELA: He said he was sorry. He promised it'd never happen again.

CARMEN: But it did. He did.

ANGELA: He doesn't mean to hurt me.

CARMEN: Right. He hits you so it'll feel good. He hits you 'cause it makes him feel good.

ANGELA: Please, don't say that.

CARMEN: Truth hurts, doesn't it?

ANGELA: He loves me. I know he loves me.

CARMEN: He loves himself.

ANGELA: We're engaged. What am I supposed to do?

CARMEN: You're engaged! Have you talked to Father Roch? Does he know about this?

ANGELA: I'm too ashamed to tell anybody.

CARMEN: Why is it the woman who's always ashamed? He's the one should be ashamed, treating you like this. Angela, you can't marry a guy who thinks you're a punching bag.

ANGELA: It'll be different when we're married.

CARMEN: It'll get worse. It always gets worse. Don't you know that?

ANGELA: What do you know about it anyway?

CARMEN: I know. Trust me. More than anybody has a right to know.

ANGELA: Oh.

CARMEN: And when you have kids. He'll punch them out too.

Even if they're little. Especially if they're little. Believe me, you don't want to marry this loser. He's *el malo. El diablo.*

ANGELA: I love him.

CARMEN: You're seventeen. What do you know about love?

ANGELA: You sound like you're ninety. What do you know about it?

CARMEN: Angela, remember that dress you wanted to buy, for your cousin's wedding?

ANGELA: The red one, with all those sequins and beads. It was a beautiful dress, wasn't it?

CARMEN: It was.

ANGELA: It was perfect.

CARMEN: Except that it didn't fit. And there was no way to ever make it fit.

ANGELA: I loved that dress. I wanted it more than anything.

CARMEN: José is like that dress. He's beautiful, wonderful, and you want him like you want the moon. But he's flawed. Terribly, terribly flawed. And nothing you can do will ever make him right. He'll never fit. Never.

ANGELA: You don't know that. He loves me. And I love him. We're going to be married as soon as I finish school. People change, you know.

CARMEN: Love, you say. Well, love isn't about hurting people to make you feel like a big man. Angela, only a coward hits women and children.

ANGELA: He's captain of the football team. He's no coward.

CARMEN: In his heart he is. And he knows exactly what he's doing when he hits you. As time goes by, he'll know even more. Where to hit you so it doesn't show. How hard to hit, so you don't break. And when he's ready to break you, he'll know exactly where and how hard.

ANGELA: Carmen, you're scaring me.

CARMEN: Good.

ANGELA: You're making a big deal out of nothing. He'll outgrow it, once we're married. He'd never treat his wife like you're talking about. Everything will be fine. Just fine. I have to go now. Got that big science test to study for. *Adios. (Exits.)*

CARMEN: *Vaya con Dios.* Little angel.

F'ever 'N Ever

(Two young women going through a pile of stuff)

SHEILA: Yours or mine?

VIV: Uh ... yours.

SHEILA: Yours. *(Puts it in a pile.)*

VIV: Mine. Yours. Mine.

SHEILA: No. I got that one when we went camping two summers ago.

VIV: OK. *(Sorts objects.)* Yours, mine. Yours. Mine. Mine. Mine. Yours.

SHEILA: I think this one's mine. But this one's yours.

VIV: Uh-unh. That one's mine.

SHEILA: You sure?

VIV: Uh-huh. I got it on that trip we took to DisneyWorld. Don't you remember? In fifth grade.

SHEILA: Sorta kinda. This is mine for sure.

VIV: No, it isn't.

SHEILA: Viv. I got that when we went canoeing.

VIV: No, Sheila. I got that for my birthday.

SHEILA: *(Takes it.)* It's mine.

VIV: *(Takes it back.)* In your wildest dreams.

SHEILA: *(Takes object.)* It's mine and you can't have it.

VIV: *(Grabs object.)* Watch my smoke, Sheila, baby. Watch my smoke.

SHEILA: *(Grabs object.)* Give it to me.

VIV: *(Tug of war)* It's mine and I'm taking it.

SHEILA: Not if I have anything to say about it.

VIV: Well, you don't.

SHEILA: *(Real struggle going on)* I wore that to Lollapalooza.

VIV: I wore it the night we watched *The Doors.*

SHEILA: *(Tugging, pulling)* That's just like you. Totally selfish.
VIV: You want everything you can get your hands on.
SHEILA: If I didn't, you'd take it all with you.
VIV: *(Circling each other, like panthers)* Of course I want to take it with me. I don't know when I'll get back. If I ever get back.
SHEILA: I hope you never come back.
VIV: Maybe I won't.
SHEILA: Promises, promises. You know you're never coming back.
VIV: I told you I'd be here Thanksgiving.
SHEILA: That's a lifetime away. Who knows where you'll be by then? Probably on Mars.
VIV: I'm only moving to Atlanta.
SHEILA: Might as well be Mars.
VIV: Look, it's not my fault my dad got a big promotion. I don't want to go either. But I have to.
SHEILA: You don't have to take all my stuff with you.
VIV: This is mine. And I'm taking it.
SHEILA: It's mine, and I'm keeping it.
VIV: You always have to have everything, don't you? All the awards, all the guys, all the ...
SHEILA: Me? You're the one who can't stand to be left out of anything. I can't even go to the bathroom without you following me.
VIV: Well, aren't you glad I'm moving?
SHEILA: Yes. I'm thrilled. I just wish you'd left a week ago.
VIV: Well, I didn't. And you're stuck with me for three more days. If you can stand it. If I can stand it.
SHEILA: I don't have to stand it. You aren't staying with me.
VIV: I am too.
SHEILA: No, you aren't.
VIV: I am. We agreed. We'd spend my last week together.
SHEILA: I don't think I can stand it.
VIV: Me either.
SHEILA: I just hate it.
VIV: Me too.
SHEILA: I don't see why it has to be this way.
VIV: Me neither.

SHEILA: You're never coming back, are you?

VIV: I don't know. I say I am, but ...

SHEILA: I know. We'll write, and then it'll dwindle down to a card or two and pretty soon you'll forget all about me.

VIV: If you don't forget about me first.

SHEILA: How can I forget my oldest and dearest?

VIV: You're my best friend. How can I ever forget you?

SHEILA: We can't. That's just it. We can't. But we will.

TOGETHER: Aaaahhhhh!!

VIV: We'll have to talk to each other every day, just like we do now.

SHEILA: You can afford to call me, but I can't. Afford a big phone bill. And besides, you'll meet all kinds of new people. Pretty soon, you'll have so many friends, all of us won't be important anymore.

VIV: Sheila. We've been friends since forever. We've been through everything together ... we'll always be friends. Forever and ever.

SHEILA: Yeah. We say that. But ...

VIV: But nothing. We just have to decide to do it. I know. E-mail.

SHEILA: On the computer I don't own.

VIV: They have 'em at school.

SHEILA: That's right. In the library.

VIV: We'll talk to each other every day. We'll set up a time.

SHEILA: It'll never work.

VIV: Would you stop being such a defeatist?

SHEILA: I can use my cousin's computer. That way we can talk at night.

VIV: See. Here. You take this.

SHEILA: No. You keep it. It really belongs to both of us.

VIV: I want you to have it.

SHEILA: I want you to have it.

VIV: I don't want it.

SHEILA: Me neither. Throw it away.

VIV: I can't believe I'm moving away. I'll miss all my friends here. All the good times we've had. The places we've been. I'll never have a better friend than you. No matter where I go or what I do.

SHEILA: Me either.

VIV: I don't want to move.

SHEILA: Me neither.
VIV: But I have to.
TOGETHER: Aaaahhhhh!!
VIV: We could tear it in two. Each take half.
SHEILA: We can have joint custody. You wear it six months, then mail it to me for six months.
VIV: Oh. OK. Or you can bring it when you come visit.
SHEILA: Or when you come visit me.
VIV: Deal.
SHEILA: Deal.
VIV: Oldest and dearest.
SHEILA: Best friends.
TOGETHER: F'ever 'n ever. Aaaaahhhhh!!

Shopping

VICTORIA: So. We'll drive to the store and you go in one door and I'll go in the other.

TRACY: I'll meet you at the lingerie counter. Only pretend we don't know each other.

VICTORIA: When you get there, I'll create a diversion, while you grab the goods.

TRACY: Right. Black lace for you. Red satin for me. Ooh. We'll be so sexy, we can't stand it.

VICTORIA: Stuff it in your purse and leave. You brought your big purse, didn't you?

TRACY: Right here. What kind of diversion?

VICTORIA: I don't know. Talk to the clerk, distract her. Knock over some stuff. I'll think of something. I'm the queen of improvisation.

TRACY: What if we get caught?

VICTORIA: No way.

TRACY: You say that, till we're sitting in jail with handcuffs.

VICTORIA: For our first offense? Anyway. So what? My Dad's a lawyer. Your dad's the mayor. What can they do to us?

TRACY: I can think of lots of things, all unpleasant.

VICTORIA: It'll be fine. Nothing's going to happen. Except that we get some sexy new lingerie our mothers would never let us buy.

TRACY: OK. Let's go.

VICTORIA: Oh. Wait a sec. I have an idea.

TRACY: What?

VICTORIA: We should hit the sports department too. I need some tennis balls.

TRACY: OK. And jewelry, too. They've got some turquoise rings to die for. Only you have to grab those.

VICTORIA: If you say so. Ready?

TRACY: Yep. We should scope out the jeans, while we're at it.

VICTORIA: And sunglasses. I lost mine.

TRACY: I need a new bathing suit. For my trip to summer camp. You game?

VICTORIA: Sure. Let's go for it. If you're gonna steal, you might as well steal big as well as small, I always say. *(Both laugh.)*

TRACY: I want a bikini.

VICTORIA: I want gold lamé.

TRACY: Better get beach towels too.

VICTORIA: And suntan oil.

TRACY: You got your big bag too?

VICTORIA: Got it. I'm ready. You?

TRACY: I'm thinking. Maybe we should wait till tomorrow, when their big sale starts. Lots of people, y'know?

VICTORIA: We already talked about that. They'll have extra security. We have to do it today.

TRACY: OK. Or we could wait till next week. When all the new stuff's in. All the really cool stuff.

VICTORIA: You sure you want to do that?

TRACY: We can go today, if you really want.

VICTORIA: Or we could go to a movie.

TRACY: What's playing?

VICTORIA: I don't know. But it's dollar day.

TRACY: I know. It's the new Batman flick. With what's his name. You got any money?

VICTORIA: I always have money.

TRACY: OK. Let's go to the show.

VICTORIA: That's cool. We can go shoplifting any time.

TRACY: We can pull our big heist next week.

VICTORIA: Or the week after.

TRACY: Actually, I'm going to summer camp next week.

VICTORIA: I'm going to visit my grandma the week after.

TRACY: So. You want to go today?

VICTORIA: No. I'd rather go to the movies.

TRACY: Me too.

VICTORIA: You buy the popcorn.

Feeling Safe

ANNA: Aren't you on the disciplinary committee of the student council?

HAPPY: I'm the chairperson.

ANNA: I've got a case for you.

HAPPY: What happened?

ANNA: I was just in the library, and ... I was actually in the video room, and ... it's just disgusting. I don't even want to talk about it.

HAPPY: Look, I gotta go to class. If you don't want to talk about it, there's nothing I can do. I'm not a mind reader.

ANNA: Wait. OK.

HAPPY: I'm late for class.

ANNA: He molested me.

HAPPY: What? Who?

ANNA: He molested me. In the video room.

HAPPY: What do you mean he molested you? Who?

ANNA: He groped me. You know. Groped. Do I have to say it?

HAPPY: I think if you're going to charge somebody with something, you have to tell what they did.

ANNA: You know what groped means, don't you?

HAPPY: He grabbed your ... Who? Who grabbed you?

ANNA: See. You can't even say it.

HAPPY: What did you do?

ANNA: I told him to get his hands off me.

HAPPY: Did he?

ANNA: Yes.

HAPPY: Oh. So, nothing happened.

ANNA: What do you mean, nothing happened? He groped me.

HAPPY: Once. I don't think that constitutes a felony.

ANNA: He touched me where I didn't want to be touched, and without my permission. Isn't that sexual harassment? I want to bring it to the committee.

HAPPY: Look. We're there for disciplinary problems, like stealing and vandalism. We aren't the sex police.

ANNA: Harry might be a mad sex fiend.

HAPPY: Harry? Harry? I doubt it.

ANNA: You don't know.

HAPPY: I know Harry. So do you. We all grew up together.

ANNA: People change.

HAPPY: Look. If you parents just got a divorce, and your sister was raped and pregnant and your grades went underground and ...

ANNA: I don't feel sorry for him.

HAPPY: I don't either. I'm just saying that fondling somebody may be a cry for love and attention.

ANNA: He's a perpetrator. You know what that is, don't you?

HAPPY: I watch *Law and Order*. Did he apologize?

ANNA: Yes. He said he didn't know what got into him. See. That means he's turning into a sex fiend. He's probably a serial rapist.

HAPPY: I think he's a little depressed, and probably confused. His grandmother died about a month ago. They were very close.

ANNA: He molested me, and I want to file a claim.

HAPPY: He said he was sorry.

ANNA: I want him to go to jail.

HAPPY: No, you don't. He's got a full scholarship to State. Something like this could stop him from going, and you know his mom can't afford to send him to college. Why don't I talk to him?

ANNA: You feel sorry for him, when I'm the one who's been damaged.

HAPPY: You're not damaged. You told him to stop, and he did. It's a non-event. He's got a bright future ahead of him, and I'm not going to ruin it for him. Harry's not a bad kid. He's just miserable. I'd be too if I was living his life. It sucks.

ANNA: When's the next meeting?

HAPPY: Next week.

ANNA: I'm coming, and I want him permanently suspended.
HAPPY: That's ridiculous.
ANNA: I want to feel safe at school. Don't you?
HAPPY: I do feel safe. Don't you think you're overreacting?
ANNA: No.
HAPPY: Well, you are.
ANNA: I don't think so.
HAPPY: You've been molested before, haven't you?
ANNA: No.
HAPPY: I don't think I believe that.
ANNA: Believe what you want.
HAPPY: You're blowing this thing way out of proportion. Something else happened to you.
ANNA: It didn't.
HAPPY: Look. Why don't we go talk to the counselor, Ms. Heiss. OK? She can help you.
ANNA: I don't want to talk to anybody.
HAPPY: I can't bring something silly like this to the committee.
ANNA: It isn't silly.
HAPPY: Poor choice of words. Try this. I'll arrange a meeting with you, me, Harry, and Ms. Heiss.
ANNA: No. Not Harry.
HAPPY: OK. You, me, and Ms. Heiss. If you want me there.
ANNA: Yes. I do. At least, to start.
HAPPY: OK.
ANNA: OK.
HAPPY: I'll set it up.
ANNA: OK.
HAPPY: OK. I gotta go. I'm late for class.
ANNA: OK.
HAPPY: OK. *(Exits.)*
ANNA: *(Breaks into tears, and exits, crying.)*

The Big Date

(Two young women dressing for a date)

GENNY: Ooh. I like that dress.

WANDA: Thanks. I like yours too. Where're you going tonight?

GENNY: A movie, I guess. You?

WANDA: A movie, probably. That's always a safe bet, for a first date with a new guy.

GENNY: Yeah. You don't have to talk very much.

WANDA: And after, you can talk about the film. *(Both laugh.)*

GENNY: First dates are always so ...

WANDA: Iffy.

GENNY: I was kind of surprised when he asked me out.

WANDA: Why? With your good looks.

GENNY: You know.

WANDA: Yeah. I wasn't surprised. I expected it. And thanks for letting me sleep over tonight.

GENNY: Oh, I'm glad you're here. I'd be too nervous by myself.

WANDA: If I'd had to go out of town with my folks, I would have had to break my date. And I wouldn't want to do that. This is like, a big deal. This guy's really something special.

GENNY: So's mine. I want it to go perfect. I could really like this guy, a lot. Oh. Be sure and be home by midnight. My folks are pretty strict about that.

WANDA: Mine too. I like that, don't you?

GENNY: It's OK. So. Where'd you meet this dream man?

WANDA: At the pool. I almost drowned when some bratty kid dive-bombed me. But my hero arrived just in time to rescue me from the circling sharks.

GENNY: Almost drowned? Girl, you're the best swimmer in town.

WANDA: But he didn't know that. How'd you meet your guy?

GENNY: Playing tennis. His ball accidentally came onto my court, and I tripped on it and almost broke my ankle.

WANDA: Accidentally on purpose, you mean.

GENNY: No. I really tripped. It hurt too.

WANDA: I meant, his ball. Wandering onto your court.

GENNY: Oh. I hadn't thought of that.

WANDA: Well, you better start thinking, girl. I'll bet you've got guys hitting on you all the time, and you don't even know it.

GENNY: You think?

WANDA: I know. So, what's this hunk of yours called?

GENNY: Paul. I forgot his last name.

WANDA: My guy's named Paul, too. It's a popular name.

GENNY: He's tall, blonde, athletic.

WANDA: Blonde. Real blonde.

GENNY: Like, almost white.

WANDA: Six feet tall at least.

GENNY: At least.

WANDA: Great tan.

GENNY: Great muscles.

WANDA: Hello. *(Pause.)*

GENNY: Hand me that perfume. Thanks.

WANDA: Let me borrow that lipstick. Thanks.

GENNY: Is that the doorbell?

WANDA: Sounds like it.

GENNY: Shall we go?

WANDA: After you. *(They walk to the door, open it.)*

TOGETHER: Hello, Paul.

WANDA: We were just leaving.

GENNY: We're going to the movies. Too bad you can't come with us.

WANDA: Maybe I'll see you around, at the pool.

GENNY: Or the tennis courts. But don't bet on it. Love.

TOGETHER: Ta ta. *(Exit.)*

Burger 'n Fries

(Two girls working in a fast food joint. They mime cooking and fixing burgers and fries. Occasionally, somebody eats a stray french fry.)

VOICE: Two big cheeses. Two fries. One chocolate shake. One punch.

KIESHA: So. What are you gonna do this weekend?

RAYNETTE: I dunno. Nothing.

KIESHA: Me neither.

RAYNETTE: Sleep, probably.

KIESHA: Me too, probably.

VOICE: One chef salad, one large fry, two cokes.

RAYNETTE: Maybe clean my room.

KIESHA: Me too.

RAYNETTE: Wanna go shopping?

KIESHA: Ain't got no money.

VOICE: Six big cheeses, six large fries, a chicken nuggets, three buffalo wings, five strawberry shakes, and five chocolate.

RAYNETTE: Me neither.

KIESHA: How 'bout a movie?

RAYNETTE: What's playing?

KIESHA: Dunno. Nothin'.

RAYNETTE: We could go skating.

KIESHA: Guess I better study. Never study during the week. Too tired.

RAYNETTE: Me too. Sure wish I didn't have to go to school.

KIESHA: Not me. I wish I didn't have to work.

RAYNETTE: I guess so. One or the other.

KIESHA: Guess so.

VOICE: Small cheese, large chicken filet, large fries and a coke.

KIESHA: I'm taking economics. You know, all about money.

RAYNETTE: I sure wish I had some.

KIESHA: Well, we sure ain't gonna make any workin' in this place.

RAYNETTE: So.

KIESHA: An' if we don't do good in school, we ain't never gonna make any.

RAYNETTE: An' working here, we ain't never gonna do good in school. Right.

KIESHA: Something's wrong, don't you think?

RAYNETTE: I'm too tired to think.

KIESHA: Me, too.

VOICE: Chicken filet, chef salad, large fry and a diet coke.

RAYNETTE: You buy your lottery ticket?

KIESHA: I forgot.

RAYNETTE: I know. Let's go play bingo.

KIESHA: Bingo?

VOICE: Three nuggets, three small fries and three diet cokes.

RAYNETTE: My aunt won a couple a hundred the other night.

KIESHA: How much it cost her?

RAYNETTE: It's only a dollar a card. But she plays lots of cards. Ten, maybe.

KIESHA: Ten dollars. To play bingo.

RAYNETTE: I guess it does sound too depressing. You and me and all the old ladies.

KIESHA: I feel like I'm as old as forever.

RAYNETTE: Me, too. Want a fry?

KIESHA: Sure, why not?

VOICE: Chocolate shake, large chocolate chip cookies, and large buffalo wings.

Forbidden Love

MIRIAM: Bekka, can I spend the night at your house tonight?

BEKKA: Sure. I guess. Your folks out of town?

MIRIAM: I wish.

BEKKA: You're seeing Tran again, aren't you? I thought your folks forbid you to see him any more.

MIRIAM: They did. But, we can't help ourselves.

BEKKA: Our own Romeo and Juliet. Don't you think ...

MIRIAM: I think I know what I'm doing. Can you help me?

BEKKA: Who am I to stand in the way of true love?

MIRIAM: Thanks. I'll be in around ...

BEKKA: Oh, I forgot. My folks are having a big party.

MIRIAM: So?

BEKKA: So, my folks are big party animals. It may last late into the night.

MIRIAM: They didn't invite my folks, did they?

BEKKA: I don't know. Probably. Don't worry about it. C'mon anyway. Have they ever met Tran? Your folks?

MIRIAM: He could be the greatest guy in the world and they still wouldn't want to hear about it.

BEKKA: All because he's Vietnamese. That's ridiculous.

MIRIAM: Tell them that. My dad's rabid. Really. He's nutty about me dating anybody who isn't ... perfect.

BEKKA: What's perfect, these days?

MIRIAM: Tran's parent's don't like it either. I'm not Catholic.

BEKKA: Oh. I've learned prejudice is a two-way street.

MIRIAM: Mom thinks I'm doing it to get back at her for who knows what. Dad thinks I'm seeing Tran to be rebellious. They even have me going to a therapist. My mom's answer to everything is to see a therapist. I told her, I can't help it that I like him. Do we ever get to choose who we fall in love with?

BEKKA: What does she say?

MIRIAM: She listens, mostly. I do all the talking. I think I'm supposed to talk myself into a solution. My parents want me to choose between them and Tran. I want to have them both. It's all a big muddle. And everybody's miserable. Me, my folks, Tran, his folks. Maybe it isn't worth it.

BEKKA: Why don't you bring him to the party tomorrow and let your folks meet him? Your dad can't go ballistic in front of a big crowd of people.

MIRIAM: You don't know my dad. Maybe I will come and bring Tran. It can't make matters worse. Can it?

BEKKA: Unless there's a big scene.

MIRIAM: With my dad, you never know.

BEKKA: Maybe we'd better forget it.

MIRIAM: Yeah. Maybe so.

BEKKA: But you should try to get them together. Your dad's only upset because he loves you and wants the best for you.

MIRIAM: As he sees it.

BEKKA: Sorry I couldn't help. But good luck.

MIRIAM: Don't worry. It'll all work out. Somehow.

Seeing Purple

(ROSIE and CARMEN sit, doing art with paper, colored pencils or pastels.)

ROSIE: Do you know what she's talking about? Talk to your picture?

CARMEN: Haven't a clue. Hand me the glue.

ROSIE: Talk to your picture? Ask what it wants? What language do we use? *(Hands her the scissors.)*

CARMEN: She's funny, isn't she? These are scissors. I need glue. *(Reaches for glue.)*

ROSIE: She's weird. Really weird. Like in strange. Odd. Bizarre. Peculiar. Eccentric. You got some green over there?

CARMEN: Yeah. *(Hands her green.)* I'm going to talk to my picture. *(Holds it up and looks at it.)* OK. Picture, tell me what you want. Oh, I feel so stupid.

ROSIE: You look stupid, too.

CARMEN: I'll get over it. Picture. Great and wonderful work of art ...

ROSIE: Right. Great and wonderful mess.

CARMEN: Hush. Oh, great and wonderful art work, tell me what you want to be.

ROSIE: You think that blank piece of paper knows more than you do?

CARMEN: She said to talk to it. Ask it what it wants. Then it'll tell me.

ROSIE: Yeah, you stupid piece of paper. Whadda ya want? You wanna be a rock, or a tree, or a ... what? A porcupine? I don't believe that.

CARMEN: It answered?

ROSIE: Yeah, but I don't know how to draw a porcupine.

CARMEN: You don't know how to draw anything.

ROSIE: So, I'm supposed to draw a porcupine? It has a lot of stickers, doesn't it?

CARMEN: I guess.

ROSIE: Look, if there's a porcupine wants to be on this paper, it's going to have to draw itself, 'cause I don't have a clue. *(Starts to draw.)* I'm not even sure what a porcupine looks like. *(Draws.)*

CARMEN: That looks pretty good.

ROSIE: It does?

CARMEN: It doesn't look much like a porcupine, but it looks good.

ROSIE: I know, but, it's supposed to be a porcupine.

CARMEN: Maybe it's an abstract porcupine.

ROSIE: Oh. Yeah. That's what it is. An abstract porcupine. *(Draws in silence.)* What have you got?

CARMEN: It sounds dumb, but, when I asked my picture what it wanted to be, it said, red. So, I'm making it red.

ROSIE: It sure is red.

CARMEN: It looks pretty good, actually.

ROSIE: You think?

CARMEN: Yeah, I do. *(They sit and draw.)*

ROSIE: This is fun, isn't it?

CARMEN: Yeah. *(They draw.)*

ROSIE: I like the way she talks about us being creative. She's a pretty neat teacher, even if she dresses kind of weird.

CARMEN: She looks like she came from some other planet where everything's magenta.

ROSIE: Artists are supposed to be different.

CARMEN: Oh, no. I made a mistake. Now it's all wrong. I've ruined my picture.

ROSIE: Art Rule number 65. Remember. There are no mistakes. Work it in. It's your chance to be creative.

CARMEN: It's so creative, it doesn't look like anything I ever saw.

ROSIE: It's its own self.

CARMEN: It is?

ROSIE: Oh, Carmen. It is good. It really is.

CARMEN: So's yours.

ROSIE: Yes. I think it is.

CARMEN: You think this works with other things, too?

ROSIE: Like what?

CARMEN: Like ... anything. Like ...

ROSIE: Like my date tonight. Ernie and I are kind of stuck in a rut, y'know? But whenever I try to shake things up, well, it sort of becomes a disaster. So, date ... what do you want to be? You decide, and let me know.

CARMEN: I've been shopping for a prom dress. They're either too this or too that or not enough of something else. I want something different. Something special. Prom dress, what do you want to be? You want to be red, or green, or peach? You want to be long or short? Sophisticated, or ... no. You don't want to be sophisticated. You want to be funky. OK. That's cool.

ROSIE: A porcupine. Who woulda ever thunk?

CARMEN: Purple. You want to be purple? I hate purple.

ROSIE: I don't need purple. But you can hand me that turquoise.

CARMEN: My dress. Purple? Are you sure? But I never wear purple.

ROSIE: *(Hands her the purple.)* You just didn't know you do.

Interview

NIKKI: Is this interview going to be taped?
HARRIET: I forgot to get batteries. I'll make notes. You ready?
NIKKI: Yes.
HARRIET: So, Nikki. How does it feel to be Student of the Month?
NIKKI: Is that the first question?
HARRIET: Yes.
NIKKI: I've never done an interview before. It's a little unnerving.
HARRIET: That's OK. It's just for the school paper. Nobody reads it. It's my first interview, too. I hope I get a scoop.
NIKKI: What's that?
HARRIET: You know. Where I get to tell the world something of importance they don't know. All reporters want to get a scoop.
NIKKI: Sounds like ice cream.
HARRIET: *(Writes.)* It feels unnerving to be Student of the Month.
NIKKI: No. That feels great. I just don't know what I did to deserve it. What did I do?
HARRIET: Nothing. I think they pulled your name out of a hat. I know that's not very encouraging.
NIKKI: I think it's great. Random choices. Just like life. Winning the lottery, getting a hit record. Student of the Month. The luck of the draw. I like it.
HARRIET: If you say so. So. What do you think about world peace?
NIKKI: I'm all for it. I like it. It's good.
HARRIET: And the economic situation?
NIKKI: I get my allowance every week. It's never enough, but my folks won't give me a raise.
HARRIET: I meant the stock market.

NIKKI: I don't know anything about it.

HARRIET: *(Writes.)* Dim view of current economic situation. OK. And the upcoming Olympics?

NIKKI: What upcoming Olympics?

HARRIET: There's always an upcoming Olympics.

NIKKI: I'd like to go.

HARRIET: *(Writes.)* Loves sports. Dreams of going to Olympics. What's your favorite event?

NIKKI: Ice skating.

HARRIET: *(Writes.)* Avid fan of the ice rink. Follows all the stars. Has pictures of Elvis and Oksana on walls at home.

NIKKI: Wait. I didn't say that. I don't have ...

HARRIET: I'm just spicing it up for reader interest. We have to make it sexy, or nobody'll pay attention. It doesn't hurt anything.

NIKKI: Whatever.

HARRIET: Do you think the President's doing a good job?

NIKKI: I never watch the news.

HARRIET: I meant the Student Body President.

NIKKI: Him? No. I don't.

HARRIET: Oh?

NIKKI: He's a do-nothing. I'm on the student council, and the meetings are a shambles. If you want a real story, go to one and see. Nothing ever gets done.

HARRIET: Who do you represent?

NIKKI: The Art Club.

HARRIET: All the flakes.

NIKKI: The creative geniuses. Listen, I could run a better meeting than he does.

HARRIET: So, you're running for Student Body President.

NIKKI: Did I say that?

HARRIET: Well, you'll probably have great posters. *(Writes.)* Artistic political rebel to challenge Prez in upcoming election.

NIKKI: What kind of interview is this? Who are you, anyway?

HARRIET: You've given me my first scoop.

NIKKI: What scoop?

HARRIET: That the student council is in chaos, the Prez is ineffective, and you're just the person to straighten out the whole mess. So. What's your platform?

NIKKI: What platform?

HARRIET: *(Writes.)* Candidate will reveal platform at upcoming press conference.

NIKKI: You're putting words in my mouth.

HARRIET: What's the first thing you'll do, when you're elected Prez?

NIKKI: Abolish the school paper.

HARRIET: You can't do that. We have freedom of the press. We have rights, you know.

NIKKI: What about my right to be quoted accurately?

HARRIET: *(Writes.)* New Prez promises to reform ...

NIKKI: And you're calling *me* a flake. I am out of here. *(Exits.)*

HARRIET: *(Writes.)* Candidate's final words. "I'm out and running." Hey. Wait up. Can I be your press secretary? *(Exits.)*

Geniuses

EMMA: That was some test, wasn't it?

BRIDGET: How'd you do?

EMMA: Missed the last question. You get it?

BRIDGET: Yes. It was easy. Better luck next time.

EMMA: I got a hundred in Science. Plus extra points for answering the essay question.

BRIDGET: I let it slide. Didn't study much. Went to a movie instead. You ever do anything besides study?

EMMA: Not much.

BRIDGET: Don't you get tired of it? I do. I hate to study.

EMMA: Doesn't matter. My Dad's determined I'm going to get into Harvard on a full scholarship.

BRIDGET: Did he go to Harvard?

EMMA: Never went to college. I guess that's why he's so fixated on me being some kind of genius. I figure if I was some kind of genius, I wouldn't have to study all the time. Wouldn't it just come natural? Seems like it does with you.

BRIDGET: I study more than I let on. Do you ever go to a movie? Or skating? Anything? Don't you want a life?

EMMA: Studying is my life. Getting good grades is my life.

BRIDGET: If I couldn't go out with my friends, I'd go bonkers. I make good grades, but not perfect grades. Mom says grades aren't everything.

EMMA: I wish she'd talk to my dad.

BRIDGET: I guess you aren't going to the prom, are you? Gee. Too bad.

EMMA: I'd really like to go.

BRIDGET: I can get you a date.

EMMA: You can? With whom? Who wants to take the class brain to the prom?

BRIDGET: I know the perfect guy. He's great. You'll have a fun time. You can even go with me and my date.

EMMA: Why are you doing this?

BRIDGET: Why not?

EMMA: Who is he?

BRIDGET: My cousin. He's out of school early and is coming to visit on his way to work at Yellowstone this summer.

EMMA: Is he cute?

BRIDGET: I don't know. I guess. He's my cousin. I love him. He's funny and smart. You'll like him.

EMMA: You think he'll want to go out with me?

BRIDGET: He'll love it. He's smart, too. You two can have a great time talking about theories of rhinoceros development or whatever.

EMMA: I don't know if my Dad will let me go. The SATs are the next weekend, and I have to make a high score.

BRIDGET: Hmmm. That's a problem.

EMMA: Maybe we better forget it.

BRIDGET: Let's use them smarts, girl. Let's us come up with a plan. What good're all these brains, if we don't use them for the important things in life?

EMMA: OK. Let's see. I'll tell him you and I are staying up all night studying for the SATs. I get dressed at your house and sleep over with you.

BRIDGET: Brilliant! I couldn't have done better myself.

EMMA: But I don't have any clothes to wear to a dance.

BRIDGET: No sweat. My sister has zillions of gowns. She's always entering beauty contests. We've got closets full.

EMMA: Does she ever win?

BRIDGET: No. But she meets lots of neat guys.

EMMA: You think it'll work?

BRIDGET: With two genuine geniuses like us? How can it fail?

Divine Love Gals of Cyberspace

(Two girls, sitting at a computer)

CHARMAINE: Aren't you in yet?

FRENCHY: Chill. OK. OK. OK!!!! I'm in.

CHARMAINE: What took you so long? Now click on ...

FRENCHY: Wow. Are we great, or are we great?

CHARMAINE: How about those guys from New Zealand and England hacking into India's nuclear information center? Even getting the pre-test e-mail from scientists from all over the world.

FRENCHY: It was OK. Except they're so nerdy. Spending their whole lives at their keyboards, withering away from lack of sun. Never meeting chicks, living on bad food. Thinking they're cool. Only geniuses like us can solve Computer 2000.

CHARMAINE: With their nerdy names. I love our name. It's just like us. It is us. Divine Love Gals of Cyberspace. Don't forget to leave our logo. We don't want people to think we're like those jerks.

FRENCHY: No guys could ever figure this out. They've been working on it for years and can't solve it. Can you imagine? Creating a computer system that doesn't read the number two! Now look what they've created. When the millennium rolls around, when we enter the year 2000, one minute after midnight, all the computers in the world will crash. Only a real nerd could come up with that system.

CHARMAINE: But do we have to remain anonymous?

FRENCHY: Fame and glory are highly overrated, so I've heard.

CHARMAINE: Say that after you've had some.

FRENCHY: OK. Let's see. Click here ... and here ... and ... no, that didn't work.

CHARMAINE: Try this. Good. Keep going.

FRENCHY: Think of it. All the governments of the world, grinding to a halt. And all the big companies. The banks, and the Pentagon and even the stores. They won't be able to take your credit cards. What will people do? They can't go shopping. Horrors. Chaos. Confusion. Muddle. Anarchy will reign supreme.

FRENCHY: My Uncle's praying the IRS goes first. They audited him last year. He hates 'em.

CHARMAINE: It's the Apocalypse. Now. Click there. No, dummy. There.

FRENCHY: And here.

CHARMAINE: And here ... good ... good ... good ... Voila!

TOGETHER: We did it! We did it!

FRENCHY: Divine Love Gals strike again.

CHARMAINE: Just another boring day. Saving the world from total ruin.

FRENCHY: Computer 2000, you are history. If they only knew how easy this is.

CHARMAINE: All we have to do now is put it out there, and ... well, you know what they say. Easy come, easy go.

FRENCHY: Are we sure we want to do this?

CHARMAINE: Do what?

FRENCHY: Save the world. Think of the possibilities. They're never going to fix this mess. Maybe it's time to let it all come down, and start all over again.

CHARMAINE: It'll be chaos. Complete, total, utter chaos. Insanity. Madness.

FRENCHY: I like it. I like it.

CHARMAINE: No you don't.

FRENCHY: Sure I do. It'll be humanity's greatest creative challenge. Think of the artistic possibilities. Talk about the new paradigm. All we have to do is sit back and let it all come crashing down.

CHARMAINE: We don't want to do that.

FRENCHY: Why not?

CHARMAINE: Because. People will get hurt. Nobody'll have a job, or food, and they'll probably lose their homes. It'll be worse than a war. Total annihilation. The end of civilization.

FRENCHY: What good's all this civilization anyway? So we can go to the mall and buy cheap junky stuff?

CHARMAINE: A lot of people will get hurt.

FRENCHY: We'll all be in the same boat, so it won't matter.

CHARMAINE: Except those with guns. You know. Those crazy survivalists and weirdos hiding out in the woods. You've seen their web pages. They have more guns than most countries. And guess who they're going to come after? You and me will be roasted marshmallows.

FRENCHY: I want chocolate on me, with coconut. If I'm gonna be eaten, I want to taste delicious.

CHARMAINE: Besides, who would be left to hack into?

FRENCHY: I guess they would come after us, with Uzis and tanks and things.

CHARMAINE: Faster'n you can click on web site number nine. *(Pause)* Frenchy, think for a second. We really do have the fate of the world in our hands.

FRENCHY: I know.

CHARMAINE: But it's real. We really have power.

FRENCHY: I know.

CHARMAINE: We could just walk away, couldn't we?

FRENCHY: We could.

CHARMAINE: Leave the world dangling. Waiting to implode. *(Pause)*

FRENCHY: OK. Let's do it. Let's save the world after all. What a drag. Let's see ... what do I do? Click here ...

CHARMAINE: And here, and no, not there ... there. Computer 2000. Prepare to meet your maker. The Divine Love Gals of Cyberspace are on the scene.

FRENCHY: Click.

Fe Fi Fo Fum

AUDREY: *(Plays violin, badly, counts.)* One, two, three, four. One, two, three, four. One two ...

MORGAN: *(Entering)* Audrey, that sounds terrible. What are you doing?

AUDREY: I'm no good, am I?

MORGAN: How long have you been playing that thing?

AUDREY: I don't play. I blunder around on the strings, hoping a decent, non-dreadful sound emerges, but it never does.

MORGAN: Maybe you should give it up.

AUDREY: Tell that to my mom. She thinks I'll get good, eventually.

MORGAN: Have you gotten better?

AUDREY: You heard me play. She's suffering from delusions.

MORGAN: How'd you get started with this? It's not like the violin's your common, ordinary, everyday musical instrument of choice.

AUDREY: Her cousin's a concert violinist. He's very famous, with people who like that stuff. I never heard of him till he came to play at the University last year and ended up at a big party at our house. Somehow, Mom got it into her head I should play the violin. Personally, I think she should take it up, but she doesn't want to hear that.

MORGAN: You used to be really good at volleyball. Why don't you go back to that?

AUDREY: You aren't hearing me. I spend all my time at violin lessons. I'm having an intensive course in misery. You should see my teacher. He's eight feet tall, weighs a billion pounds and looks like a frog.

MORGAN: Sounds charming.

AUDREY: I talked to my dad, and told him this whole enterprise was an exercise in emotional, creative, and financial bankruptcy.

But he told me to stick with it. I thought he'd be sympathetic. He hates listening to me practice. Every time Mom makes me break out the violin, he runs out of the house on some emergency errand. This whole thing is ruining our family togetherness.

MORGAN: Can I play your violin?

AUDREY: Better than me, probably.

MORGAN: *(Plays.)* This is fun.

AUDREY: As much fun as a toxic dump.

MORGAN: I like it. I'm not playing anything. But I sure like the way it feels and sounds. This bow is pretty impressive. Maybe you should change your attitude.

AUDREY: What? From hopeless to total despair?

MORGAN: I don't know. That's what I do when I have to do something I hate. Change my attitude. You could pretend you're a famous violinist.

AUDREY: I don't want to be a famous violinist.

MORGAN: There must be something to like about it.

AUDREY: Standing there, week after week with my teacher is not to like. He counts — One, two, three, fo. He can't even say four. One, two, three, fo. One, two, three, fo. Sounds like fe fi fo fum, and I'm the blood of the Englishman.

MORGAN: I think you're really lucky. Not many people get to play the violin.

AUDREY: Not many people want to. And besides, I told you. I don't play. I wander around lost praying I'll stumble onto a melody before one, two, three, fo drives me insane.

MORGAN: *(Returns violin.)* Well, good luck. I gotta go to soccer.

AUDREY: *(Hands her violin.)* Here.

MORGAN: I can't take that.

AUDREY: Please. You like it. Take it.

MORGAN: No way. Your mama'd kill both of us. Bye. *(Exits.)*

AUDREY: Bye. *(Plays.)* Fe fi fo fum. Fe fi fo fum. Fe fi fo fum. Fe fi fo fum. Fe fi fiddley dee. Tra la tra la tra la tra la. I am ze gypsy violinist. Tra la tra la tra la. Ze gypsy fortune teller violinist. Ze brilliant and beautiful gypsy fortune teller violinist. How can anybody be so bad? *(Walks past garbage can. Tosses violin and bow in can, exits.)* Tra la tra la tra la tra la.

The Last Ice-Cream Cone

TONI: Gee, Mary. You look like you just lost your best friend. What's the matter?

MARY: Oh. Toni. I just came from the doctor.

TONI: Not good?

MARY: It could be worse.

TONI: You want to talk about it? C'mon. I'll buy you an ice cream and we can talk about it.

MARY: I've had my last ice cream cone.

TONI: It's not that fattening.

MARY: It's the sugar. I just found out I'm ... *(Pause)*

TONI: My aunt's a diabetic. She eats sugar-free ice cream. You can have one of those.

MARY: No thanks. It's too depressing to even think about.

TONI: I'm really sorry.

MARY: No sugar. No cokes or candy bars. No alcohol. I have to give myself shots every day. And I could go blind.

TONI: Ouch.

MARY: And I probably can't have children. I might as well kill myself. Who's ever going to want to marry me? What kind of life can I have?

TONI: My aunt has a good life. She travels all over the country. She has a great job.

MARY: Does she have children?

TONI: She always said she never wanted them. Snot-nosed little brats, she calls them.

MARY: She just says that so she won't feel so bad.

TONI: Her husband doesn't seem to mind that they don't have kids.

MARY: I bet her heart's broken. Mine is. I always wanted kids. Lots of kids.

TONI: Think of all those kids out there waiting for you to adopt them.

MARY: It isn't the same.

TONI: You really feel bad, don't you?

MARY: Yeah. I feel ... hopeless. Lost and hopeless. I have a chronic illness. Chronic. That means forever. I can't even think how to behave. Like, at graduation, everybody'll be toasting with champagne, while I'll be drinking a diet whatever.

TONI: You can probably have a career as the designated driver.

MARY: Wow. What a thrill.

TONI: At least you won't become an alcoholic.

MARY: Too bad.

TONI: I know you feel pretty low right now. But you'll learn to live with it. Millions of people do.

MARY: I don't want to be millions of people.

TONI: You already are. Just as I am. I'm the millions of people who don't have diabetes. Look. I understand.

MARY: No, you don't. This isn't fun, and I'm not going to pretend it is. I hate it. I just hate it. It's the end of the world. Worse. It's the descent into hell to meet the devil himself. And all his demons and dragons. It's a walk through fire. A fall into a river of ice. A bottomless pit with ten thousand snakes waiting at the bottom, writhing with glee that I'm to be their next meal. It's being attacked by wild beasts. It's being gnawed and chewed up and dismembered and eaten alive.

TONI: There. You feel better.

MARY: No. I feel horrible.

TONI: Good. Are you ready for some really yummy ice cream now?

MARY: You think they have sugar-free chocolate?

TONI: Probably. Hey. You'll probably have the best figure of anybody in school. Think of all the great clothes you can wear. And how everybody will hate you because you're so gorgeous.

MARY: Oh, shut up.

TONI: Right.

Runaways

TONYA: You been out on your own long?

HUMMINGBIRD: Long enough.

TONYA: Know any place to crash tonight? A shelter or something?

HUMMINGBIRD: You can crash at my pad. I got a lumpy sofa you can sleep on.

TONYA: Thanks. I'll take it.

HUMMINGBIRD: What's your name?

TONYA: Tonya. What's yours?

HUMMINGBIRD: Hummingbird.

TONYA: Oh. That's not your real name, is it?

HUMMINGBIRD: It is now. You aren't looking to get any reward money, are you?

TONYA: No. Why?

HUMMINGBIRD: My folks got a thousand bucks out for info on me. For my safe return.

TONYA: Gee. A thousand dollars. Your folks must be rich.

HUMMINGBIRD: They buy whatever they want.

TONYA: Maybe you should go back home, if they want you that bad. Why'd you leave home? Why'd you run away?

HUMMINGBIRD: I'd rather be swallowed by pythons than go back home.

TONYA: Bad, huh?

HUMMINGBIRD: What about you? You just arrived, on the scene.

TONYA: It's kinda scary, being out on your own, with nothing.

HUMMINGBIRD: Where you from?

TONYA: Down south. Alabama.

HUMMINGBIRD: A southern belle. Honey chile, I hope you don't get eaten alive.

TONYA: So. What do you do for money?

HUMMINGBIRD: Oh. The usual.

TONYA: You mean ... you don't mean ... not ...

HUMMINGBIRD: I beg, borrow, steal. Actually, I pick up work from a lady I know. She runs a clinic and lets me do some typing when they need extra help for reports and things. It's not steady, but helps me keep off the curb at night.

TONYA: I was hoping to get a restaurant job.

HUMMINGBIRD: You probably can.

TONYA: I waited tables back home.

HUMMINGBIRD: Why'd you run away?

TONYA: The usual.

HUMMINGBIRD: Your old man ...

TONYA: He's pretty violent. When my mom ran off, he came after me with a butcher knife. I fled for my life and haven't looked back.

HUMMINGBIRD: A butcher knife. That can be hazardous to your health.

TONYA: Actually it was a meat cleaver. He's a butcher.

HUMMINGBIRD: Sounds like a real wacko.

TONYA: So, here I am homeless and looking for a job. Actually, I'm hoping to connect with some musicians. I plan on becoming a major rock super star.

HUMMINGBIRD: Oh yeah. Can you sing?

TONYA: *(Sings.)*

HUMMINGBIRD: I know a guy, plays with a band. They're looking for back-up. Maybe I could introduce you.

TONYA: Sure.

HUMMINGBIRD: We can call him when we get home. You got any money? I want to stop and get something for supper.

TONYA: Sure. And you'll call your friend. What's the name of his band?

HUMMINGBIRD: Who knows. The Radical Scorpion Punks from Outer Space. I'll call him, soon's we get home. How much money you got?

TONYA: Look. I think I'll pass. Thanks anyway, but, I'll see you around. *(Runs off.)*

HUMMINGBIRD: Hey. Come back. I really do have a friend y'know. I really do.

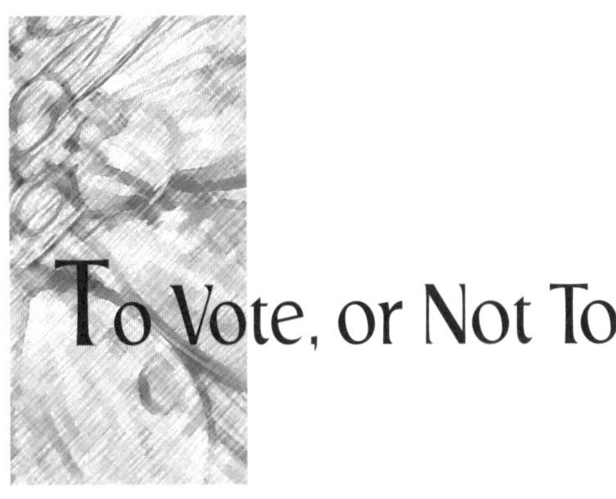

To Vote, or Not To

BETSY: Come on. You have to come. It's our first time.

ERIN: No. I'm not going.

BETSY: Do you know how many people never get to vote? For anything. Look at all those people in China. They'd love to be able to vote on things.

ERIN: We aren't in China.

BETSY: You're sure in a bad mood.

ERIN: You go vote. I'll meet you later, at the gym or something.

BETSY: I don't want to go by myself. This is our very first election. It's a big deal.

ERIN: Just 'cause we registered, doesn't mean we have to vote. It's an option, isn't it? Nobody's going to arrest us if we don't. And don't give me all that history class malarkey about life, liberty and the pursuit of happiness. That's political mumbo jumbo somebody made up to impress the masses.

BETSY: What's the matter with you? And don't tell me you're having a bad hair day. Something's really bothering you. What is it? Love, liberty or the pursuit of ...

ERIN: Leave me alone. Go vote.

BETSY: Larry dumped you, right?

ERIN: I knew it was coming. I shouldn't be so surprised.

BETSY: That's no excuse not to vote. Boyfriends come and go but ...

ERIN: Democracy never dies. How patriotic.

BETSY: OK. But when the dictator's troops are banging down your door to arrest you for drinking coffee without a permit, don't complain.

ERIN: Stop.

BETSY: And when they've got you in jail for writing a letter to your best friend ...

ERIN: You're boring me.

BETSY: And when they have you on the rack, trying to make you confess to ...

ERIN: All right. I'll go vote. But you have to buy dinner.

BETSY: I will not. That's bribery.

ERIN: That's politics. Trade you my vote on the highway bill for a steak dinner. With dessert.

BETSY: Let's go, before the polls close.

ERIN: Who are you voting for?

BETSY: You know it's secret.

ERIN: Not like secret secret.

BETSY: Yes. Secret secret.

ERIN: You're dragging me to the polls and won't even tell me who you're voting for. How else will I know who not to vote for?

BETSY: Haven't you watched TV? The election's been all over the news. Or were you too busy with Larry to pay attention?

ERIN: I'm glad Larry dumped me. Not totally. I have a few atoms of pride in this body. But I knew it wasn't going to work out. Now I'm free to go on to somebody else. Oh. Now I remember. Somebody died. That's why they're having an election.

BETSY: My neighbor's running for city council.

ERIN: And you're voting for him. Oh. I forgot. Secret.

BETSY: No. It's OK. Yes. I am voting for him. He's a nice man. I like his son, too. He just came home from college. He's a hunk.

ERIN: So you're voting for the old man so you can make it with the son. What kind of democracy is that?

BETSY: No, no. He's really a good guy. He'll make a great councilman. You should vote for him.

ERIN: OK. If you'll introduce me to his son.

BETSY: Erin. Don't vote.

ERIN: You couldn't stop me now.

Jealousy Becomes You

PENNY: My hair's so awful. I wish mine was like yours. All curly and pretty.

BONNIE: Are you blind? My hair hasn't been cut in six weeks and this perm is totally fried.

PENNY: Oh, and look at my shoes. They're so scuffed and frumpy. I'd get new ones, but I'm so broke I couldn't buy a broken glass at a garage sale.

BONNIE: I don't even carry a purse anymore. Why bother, when it's always empty?

PENNY: Didn't you baby-sit last week?

BONNIE: That money was spent years ago. Have you studied for English? I guess I'll get my usual F.

PENNY: I thought you were doing good.

BONNIE: I wish.

PENNY: Me, too. Know what Mr. Sims did, on our algebra test? He wrote a problem on the board and then told the class he put it up so I'd get at least one question right. Know what it was? $2 + 2 = X$.

BONNIE: Did you get it right?

PENNY: It was the only one I did get.

BONNIE: I failed history, too.

PENNY: I didn't get picked for the girl's chorus.

BONNIE: I bombed out at cheerleader tryouts.

PENNY: My mom won't let me go with her to my cousin's wedding.

BONNIE: My dad made me leave home when his boss came to dinner.

PENNY: That sucks. *(Pause)* Gee, I sure like your fingernail polish.

BONNIE: This ugly stuff? It's hideous. I can't wait to get rid of it.

PENNY: My nails look like I've been digging in a minefield.

BONNIE: They look pretty good to me. Maybe a little long.

PENNY: Long? They're not long at all. I'd give anything to have nice long nails like yours.

BONNIE: You don't want nails like mine.

PENNY: Yes, I do.

BONNIE: No, you don't.

PENNY: I most certainly do.

BONNIE: That's just like you.

PENNY: What?

BONNIE: You're always so jealous. As soon as you think anybody has anything the least bit better than you, you turn green with envy and make life miserable for everybody.

PENNY: I'm not jealous.

BONNIE: Yes, you are.

PENNY: I am not.

BONNIE: You are too.

PENNY: Jealous of what? Your tacky clothes? If anything, you're jealous of me.

BONNIE: Of what? Your sparkling personality?

PENNY: Yes. And my good taste. And my boyfriend.

BONNIE: What's his name? Forget it. That guy's the biggest loser in town.

PENNY: Oh yeah. Well, no male in his right mind would be seen with you, even with a paper bag over his head.

BONNIE: I'll have you know, *you know who* asked me for a date this weekend.

PENNY: In your wildest dreams.

BONNIE: Yeah. Well, he's taking me to the game Friday night. You'll see.

PENNY: Look, you don't have to make up stories to make yourself look good. Jealousy does not become you, Bonnie.

BONNIE: Me, jealous? Of you? That's like envying Godzilla.

PENNY: Godzilla should look so good.

BONNIE: At least all my clothes don't smell like a sewer. *(Pause)* No, they don't.

PENNY: They don't.

BONNIE: No. They smell like a toxic dump.

PENNY: You are so jealous.

BONNIE: OK. I'm jealous.

PENNY: I knew it.

BONNIE: I mean, who wouldn't be? With your beautiful skin and great figure.

PENNY: Me? I don't have a great figure. And my skin's so bad I look like I've broken out with ebola.

BONNIE: Yeah. But at least you've got beautiful feet.

PENNY: You call these beautiful? I call 'em monster claws.

BONNIE: You're right. They're pretty awful.

PENNY: What?

BONNIE: Your feet. They're pretty bad.

PENNY: Well. At least I have pretty hands.

BONNIE: If you say so.

PENNY: And rings. See.

BONNIE: Yep. They're pretty great.

PENNY: Now, if I just had a new lipstick.

BONNIE: You know what they say.

PENNY: No. What?

BONNIE: You can't have everything.

Pheasant, Rabbit, or Me

ABRA: *(Reading cookbook)* This sounds good. Roast pheasant in sauterne wine with mushrooms and parsley. Wild rice pilaf and buttered carrots with mint.

TRUDY: It sound like a year's allowance.

ABRA: Too fancy, you think?

TRUDY: It is a bit exotic.

ABRA: I like exotic.

TRUDY: I don't see why you don't barbeque hamburgers. Guys love hamburgers.

ABRA: He can get a hamburger a zillion places. I want to fix him something special.

TRUDY: You're not thinking of marrying this guy, are you?

ABRA: Maybe. When we both grow up. Anyway, I want him to like me and Mom says the best way to a man's heart is ...

TRUDY: Through his stomach. I've heard that all my life.

ABRA: Dad agrees. He always says he married Mom for her meatloaf and mashed potatoes.

TRUDY: My dad's favorite is chicken pot pie. Why don't you fix Frankie something like that?

ABRA: I don't know how to make chicken pot pie.

TRUDY: You don't know how to make pheasant with whatever either. If it were me, I'd open a jar of Ragu and forget it.

ABRA: You're never going to get married, with that attitude.

TRUDY: I'll marry a chef and let him do the honors.

ABRA: This looks good. Braised rabbit with rosemary and Parmesan cheese. I wonder what braised means.

TRUDY: You're not going to eat a poor little rabbit, are you?

ABRA: It's no worse than a poor little chicken. Oh here. Pork chops with garlic and ginger.

TRUDY: That'll drive him away. Don't you think you're a bit over the top with this? If you have to con some guy into liking you because you can make a turkey souffle, you'll spend your whole life in the kitchen washing dishes. Whatever happened to love and devotion and, horrors, the S word.

ABRA: Cooking is a highly creative art form. You should cultivate it.

TRUDY: It's drudgery and you know it. You just have the hots for this guy and will stop at nothing to get him. Even killing defenseless rabbits.

ABRA: You get them out of the freezer at the grocery store.

TRUDY: Why can't your good looks and sparkling personality be enough?

ABRA: The competition's hot and heavy out there, in case you haven't noticed. You have to use every little thing to get an edge.

TRUDY: But, the Easter bunny? Look. It's not like when our folks were getting married. We live in a different world. Men and women are like, equal. When I get married, we're going to eat out at every meal. My husband will love and adore me and worship me as the goddess I am, whether I can cook or not.

ABRA: How about duck a l'orange? That sounds tasty.

TRUDY: How about a peanut butter sandwich?

Talk to the Trees

JAN: Let's go inside. It's getting hot out here.

LAUREL: Let's sit under this tree. It's nice and shady and we can work.

JAN: But if it gets hot, we're going inside. Deal.

LAUREL: Deal. But it'll be nice. You'll see. Trees can handle everything.

JAN: Sure. That tree over there, it's gonna do my science report. The Search for Alien Intelligence in the Universe. That sounds like a Jodie Foster movie.

LAUREL: That tree has more brains than half the population.

JAN: What's it gonna do, figure out how to pay the national debt?

LAUREL: It might. It also might save your life one day.

JAN: How? It just sits there.

LAUREL: Suppose we were stranded on a desert island. We could cut it down and make a boat.

JAN: If we had a chain saw. And last time I looked, desert islands didn't come furnished with hot and cold running electricity. So. They have all these satellites out in the desert, trying to find extra-terrestrial intelligence out there in the cosmos. *(Speaks gibberish space language.)*

LAUREL: I'm going to write my report on the intelligence of trees.

JAN: You're going to get an F. You know he wants this to be about aliens and spaceships and stuff. The Hubble telescope. All that. If he wanted a report about trees, he'd tell us. Trees aren't intelligent. They're just trees.

LAUREL: Just because they don't have brains that look like ours doesn't mean they don't have brains. Theirs may be in their seeds, or leaves, or roots. They even talk to each other, telling the other trees about pests and diseases in the forest. *(Speaks gibberish tree language.)*

JAN: I guess they have feelings too. Like, it hurts when you prune them or whatever. Ouch, you're hurting me, giving my branches that manicure. Get real.

LAUREL: We used to have a big pecan tree outside the kitchen. It was at least sixty feet tall, and big and shady. Every season we got hundreds and hundreds of pecans off of it. My Dad and I always made fudge for Christmas, with the pecans. But the leaves were ruining the roof, so my folks decided to cut it down. I came home from school one day and the tree was gone. It was like total emptiness. All the leaves were gone. All the shade. The trunk was gone too, that I'd seen a zillion times a day, every day of my life when I went in and out the back door. All that was left was a stump. The stump was oozing sap, like it was bleeding, or crying. It hurt my heart so bad, to look at it, I cried, too.

JAN: I didn't think trees could cry.

LAUREL: Everybody in the family was so sad that night. Nobody could eat any supper. All we did was sit around and think about the pecan tree. How it'd been a part of our lives since forever, and now it was gone. I felt like I'd lost an old, dear friend.

JAN: You could plant another one.

LAUREL: I'd be a mother myself before another tree grew that tall again. Maybe even a grandmother.

JAN: Oh.

LAUREL: Since then, nobody goes out the back door any more, it hurts so bad. Dad says he'll never cut down another tree. Better to fix the roof every year than kill a tree. Mom says she feels like a murderer.

JAN: Gee.

LAUREL: I think we're going to move. Dad says he wants to find a place in the country.

JAN: With lots of trees, huh?

LAUREL: I guess.

JAN: Do you think flowers have brains too?

LAUREL: I think everything does. Whether it's in outer space, or in the backyard.

JAN: I think space is exciting. I hope there is life out there, and we get to meet it one day. Learn space talk. *(Speaks gibberish space language.)* Neat-O. I can get into that.

LAUREL: I hope you do. Me. I'll be happy just to figure out how to talk to the trees. *(Speaks gibberish tree language.)*

The Cave

(Two girls, in a cave, with flashlights)

AMBER: It's very dark in here. I can't see a thing.

EBONY: Caves are dark. They don't have windows. That's why we brought flashlights.

AMBER: I'll bet there's creepy crawlies in here. I hate creepy crawlies.

EBONY: They don't like you either.

AMBER: What did I just step in? It's not that bat stuff, is it?

EBONY: Amber, we're having an intimate encounter with Mother Earth. Would you please stop griping?

AMBER: Look, I'm your city cousin, remember? I'm not used to crawling around in the dark, stepping in bat stuff. Why are we even doing this?

EBONY: Look at that formation.

AMBER: Looks like a big mushroom.

EBONY: It's a stalagmite.

AMBER: Is that the one that grows from the top or the bottom?

EBONY: Bottom. That one's a baby. Probably only a couple of million years old.

AMBER: How far do we have to go?

EBONY: For what?

AMBER: To find something interesting.

EBONY: Don't you think it's interesting, just being in this dark hole in the planet?

AMBER: My feet hurt.

EBONY: This cave isn't for your entertainment pleasure, cuz.

AMBER: Oh, Ebony. Don't be such a jerk. You talked me into this, and I'm trying to be a good sport about it.

EBONY: You only promised to come if I promised to go to the beach with you. So you can work on your tan. And fish for guys.

AMBER: Oh, I love the sun. It feels so warm and good on your skin. And the sound of the waves, breaking on the beach. It just lulls me to sleep like nothing else. I love it so much. And what's wrong with fishing for guys?

EBONY: Gives you skin cancer. I'll have to wear a ton of sun screen.

AMBER: Fishing for guys?

EBONY: No, dummy. Sunbathing.

AMBER: Don't you like to meet good looking guys?

EBONY: Sure. I said I'd go, didn't I? I just don't like being out in the sun. It's hot, and the sand gets in your bathing suit and itches.

AMBER: One day of sun worshiping won't hurt you.

EBONY: OK. We're coming up to the cathedral.

AMBER: I never go to church. Do you?

EBONY: Try and be open to the experience, Amber.

AMBER: I'm trying. I'm trying. How much longer, till we get there?

EBONY: You sound like my little brother, on summer vacation. We're almost there.

AMBER: Good. Can we turn around then, and go back out? How'd you ever get into this anyway? You have to admit it's a rather unusual hobby, tunneling through caves.

EBONY: My dad started taking me exploring with him when I was a little girl. We don't get to go very much anymore, he's so busy at work. Oh. We're almost there. Here. I brought extra flashlights. Take this. And shine them, up on the walls. It'll take a minute for your eyes to get used to the light. Stay with it, OK. First time I came here, I thought I'd discovered the meaning of life.

AMBER: *(Gasps.)* This is incredible. It is like a cathedral. Only better. Nobody's preaching at you.

EBONY: Shhhhhh.

AMBER: But it's so beautiful. I've never seen anything like it.

EBONY: Shhhhhh.

AMBER: Look at that stalactite. It's like a dancer, leaping through the air.

EBONY: SHHHHHH!
AMBER: Why? Is something wrong?
EBONY: Shhhhh.

(Both become totally still and silent. A silence so deep, so profound, it defies words. If felt by the players, it will be felt by the audience. All lines are now whispered, or extremely quiet.)

AMBER: Gee. Thanks, cuz. For bringing me here.
EBONY: You ready to go?
AMBER: Shhh.

(Both sit down, and are soon lost in the silence of the earth.)

The Creek

(Two girls, with baskets, in the woods)

CLARA: Thanks, Nicole, for helping me pick the wildflowers. I think they'll be perfect, don't you?

NICOLE: I just wish they lasted longer. They're so fragile.

CLARA: I know. I feel kind of guilty picking them for a party. But they're so beautiful, I want everybody to enjoy them.

NICOLE: The flowers aren't here for our enjoyment, you know. Anyway, I don't think you need to worry. We haven't seen any flowers yet.

CLARA: I haven't seen very many birds either, have you? Or butterflies? They're usually out this time of year, migrating to South America. Maybe it's early.

NICOLE: So, who's coming to the party? Not any geeks, I hope.

CLARA: Would I have geeks at my party?

NICOLE: Look.

CLARA: Where?

NICOLE: Over there, by the creek. What is that?

CLARA: I don't know. What?

NICOLE: It looks like, oh crud.

CLARA: I smell it. Don't go over there, Nicole. Wait. Come back. For heaven's sake, don't touch it.

NICOLE: How could they do that?

CLARA: What is it? Not a dead body, I hope.

NICOLE: Somebody dumped who knows what in the creek.

CLARA: Get away from it. You don't think it's toxic, do you?

NICOLE: I don't know. It could be. People dump all kinds of things in all kinds of places. I saw a story on TV about a cruise ship company that had to pay a huge fine because they had all their ships dumping oil in the ocean. Isn't that disgusting? They did it on purpose. I'm glad they got caught.

CLARA: What do we do?

NICOLE: Don't touch it. It may be nuclear.

CLARA: We don't have any nuclear plants around here.

NICOLE: They cart that stuff all over the country.

CLARA: I guess we have to call the police.

NICOLE: My dad's in the Sierra Club. He'll know what to do.

CLARA: This hurts me so much, to see people doing things like this, in our own town.

NICOLE: I guess it's everywhere.

CLARA: No wonder we didn't see any birds. They're either dead or fled.

NICOLE: Maybe the groundwater's polluted too, and that's why we didn't find any wildflowers.

CLARA: Do you think we're being poisoned, by standing here? We better leave.

NICOLE: We have on shoes. We should be safe.

CLARA: I don't care. I'm getting out of here. That stuff really stinks. I wonder what it is. It's disgusting.

NICOLE: Wait up.

CLARA: What?

NICOLE: I think I'm going to vomit. *(Retches.)*

CLARA: I think we should go see the doctor.

NICOLE: We can tell the TV station, and the newspaper, and make a big deal out of it.

CLARA: It really is a big deal, isn't it? Are you all right?

NICOLE: I hope so. It would be too cruel if a pleasant walk in the country turned into a long stay in the hospital. *(Retches.)* Or worse.

CLARA: I've just never been one to get involved in causes. People think you're a nut.

NICOLE: But, there's ways and then there's ways, to get involved. I'm going to talk to my dad and see what he says.

CLARA: My mom has a friend who's a lawyer. He's always taking on causes, and people like him. I like him.

NICOLE: I'm going to join that club at school. The Nature Club.

CLARA: But those kids are all such geeks.

NICOLE: Maybe it's time we all became geeks.

CLARA: Oh no. I'll do anything but become a geek.

NICOLE: Look, I really don't feel very good. That stuff has given me a headache. Let's go home. You drive.

CLARA: Maybe I should take you to the hospital.

NICOLE: No. Take me home. My mom will know what to do.

CLARA: I'm scared. What if we're all contaminated. You sure you don't want to go to the hospital?

NICOLE: And tell them what? We don't even know what that stuff is.

CLARA: I'm not going to collect any samples. I like my life too much.

NICOLE: I feel terrible. *(Retches.)*

CLARA: I'll call your mom on the way, and she can meet us at the hospital. *(They exit.)*

Easy Come, Easy Go

BRIDGET: You look like you just lost your best friend.
CARA: I'm just reading this book.
BRIDGET: What are you reading?
CARA: *Gone With the Wind.* You ever read it?
BRIDGET: I saw the movie. Made me cry. *Sic transit gloria.*
CARA: What's that mean?
BRIDGET: Glory fades. Here today, gone tomorrow. Something like that. C'mon. Lemme buy you a pizza, OK? It'll make you feel better.
CARA: No thanks.
BRIDGET: I'm spending my inheritance. My aunt died and left me some money. I'm an heiress.
CARA: Great.
BRIDGET: Well, gee. It isn't a huge fortune, but I can afford to buy you a pizza.
CARA: *(Bows her head.)*
BRIDGET: Cara, you're crying. What is it, Cara? What's the matter?
CARA: *(Cries.)*
BRIDGET: You want me to get you some water?
CARA: *(Cries quietly.)*
BRIDGET: You want to talk about it?
CARA: No. Yes. No. I mean, it's ... it's too ... I ...
BRIDGET: When things are that bad, you need to tell somebody.
CARA: You know my dad died a year ago.
BRIDGET: In that boating accident, out at the lake.
CARA: Yeah. *Sic transit gloria.* Where'd you learn that, anyway?
BRIDGET: My grandfather. He's a judge and knows great Latin

stuff. *Carpe diem*. That means to enjoy life. Whatever.

CARA: Well, I never told anybody this, but my dad left me a lot of money.

BRIDGET: You're an heiress too. Don't you love that word, heiress? It makes me feel so rich. I'm not really, but it is fun. Are you rich? I mean, really rich?

CARA: *Sic transit gloria.*

BRIDGET: I don't get it.

CARA: My mom was supposed to be helping me invest it. And it's a lot, too. A whole lot.

BRIDGET: I hope you're not going to say what I think you're going to say.

CARA: I just came from seeing a lawyer. That's what happens when you get money. You get lawyers too. And judges, too, probably. Maybe I'll get your granddad.

BRIDGET: This doesn't sound very good.

CARA: I've been applying to colleges. But when I asked for the money to send in deposits ... And that's not all. Since I got the inheritance, my mom's been making me pay rent, buy all my own food and clothes, plus she charges me a monthly management fee. I've been paying her to steal my money. And she has a great job. It's not like we're homeless or starving. Or even poor. We aren't. Well, I am now. I'm not only poor. I'm homeless. 'Cause I sure can't go back and live with her.

BRIDGET: I don't know what to say. "Easy come, easy go" pops to mind. That's a cousin to *sic transit gloria*. That probably isn't very helpful.

CARA: Somebody steals a hundred zillion dollars, and I'm supposed to just let it go, like it's nothing?

BRIDGET: It's just paper. Actually, it's pizza.

CARA: At first I thought that money was a blessing. But it isn't. It's a curse.

BRIDGET: My inheritance isn't big, like yours. It's just enough to help get me through college with a movie now and then. But at least I won't have to work in some fast food joint, or pile up student loans I'll be paying back forever. And it's bought me some pretty good things, too. My trip to Outward Bound, and

Mexico to see the pyramids. But Mom didn't make me pay rent, or buy all my clothes. She doesn't take a management fee, although my granddad said she could. What are you going to do?

CARA: Find a place to live. Try to, anyway. Without any money, I don't know.

BRIDGET: Don't you have any aunts or uncles? What about your grandmother?

CARA: She said I could come live with her. But she's three hundred miles away. I want to stay here and finish school.

BRIDGET: Right now, you're coming home with me.

CARA: Why'd she do it? Why'd my mom steal my money? I'm her only child. How could she do this to me? Doesn't she love me?

BRIDGET: People get weird about money.

CARA: Weird? As in G-R-E-E-D.

BRIDGET: I'm sure she loves you, but she's probably scared.

CARA: Scared? Of what?

BRIDGET: I don't know. But adults are always afraid about money. Afraid there's not enough. My mom gets like that. I sometimes think being an adult isn't much fun. They're always worried about something. Mostly money.

CARA: Do you think I'll ever get it back? I mean, how could she have spent that much in such a short time?

BRIDGET: You want pepperoni or mushrooms? Hey, we can splurge, and have both.

CARA: OK.

BRIDGET: In fact, let's order the works. Yeah. We can get the works.

CARA: It's your money. Easy come, easy go.

BRIDGET: Maybe we should just get pepperoni.

CARA: Whatever.

BRIDGET: Actually, we should probably get cheese. They have a special on cheese today, don't they? That's it. We'll get cheese.

CARA: *Sic transit* pizza.

Hurricane Force

GALE: *(Standing outside, obviously enjoying herself. A strong wind blows.)*

EARTHA: Gale, you better come inside now. The wind's really picking up.

GALE: Oh, Eartha. Don't you just love it? Blow wind blow. Hit me with your best shot.

EARTHA: We've got to get home, to get ready.

GALE: But it feels so good, blowing through my hair. And on my skin. Nothing feels better than the wind. It's like little kisses from Mother Nature.

EARTHA: You're crazy. There's a terrible storm coming, and we've got to get home. Now, come on before I drag you.

GALE: Next thing you'll be telling me we have to evacuate.

EARTHA: We might. And we have to be ready.

GALE: Oh, you're right. But can't we stay out just a few more minutes? It's not that bad yet.

EARTHA: No.

GALE: Ever since I was a little girl, I've loved to be outside in hurricanes, with the wind and the rain.

EARTHA: I remember that time you had me tie you to the tree so you could be out in the worst of it. I'll never forget that spanking. I've never seen Daddy so mad. He thought you were dead. So he spanks me.

GALE: It sure was fun.

EARTHA: Speak for yourself. I hope we go to Aunt Susies to weather the storm and watch the hurricane on TV. Those are some of the funnest times of our lives, aren't they?

GALE: Everybody there, all the aunts and uncles, cousins and in-laws. Hurricanes are the only time the whole family gets together, except for funerals.

EARTHA: Mom always makes spaghetti, Aunt Susie has a bathtub full of sodas, Uncle James brings smoked turkey and Uncle Rory drives everybody crazy telling us about his latest guru.

GALE: Remember the time he brought that swami to the hurricane? What a creep. Pretending to find a gold ring in my hair. Even I could see through that trick.

EARTHA: You mean it wasn't real?

GALE: Ahhhhh. It must be up to about 30 miles an hour now. Fabulous. Simply fabulous.

EARTHA: I'm going home now, Gale. If you get stuck here, don't blame me.

GALE: I'm coming. Anyway, you can't drive. You don't have your license.

EARTHA: You remember the time when we had to go stay in that bomb shelter?

GALE: Yeah. When we were on vacation at the beach and the storm came up and they made us go to that old army bunker at the fort. That was a trip. Like being in a movie.

EARTHA: I don't like storms. They make me nervous. So, come on. We have to go home and help mom with the spaghetti.

GALE: It must be close to 40 now. Think it'll get to 100? Maybe even 125.

EARTHA: Come on. You're making me crazy.

GALE: Oh, don't be such a scaredy cat. We're safe. Nothing's going to happen. Just feel the wind. Be with it. One with the wind, the earth, the sky.

EARTHA: You're going to get in big trouble one day, doing crazy things like this. You're going to get hurt.

GALE: Mother Nature having a fit. A first rate temper tantrum. Blowing and screaming and raining down like cats and dogs. I love it. I just love it. Makes me feel so alive. All that energy swirling around. And I know when to stop. When to come in out of the wind.

EARTHA: I'm going now. With you or without you, license or not,

I'm going home.

GALE: I'm coming.

EARTHA: You better hurry.

GALE: Fifty miles per hour. Go, wind go.

EARTHA: Goodbye. And I have the keys, and I know how to drive. *(Exits.)*

GALE: Eartha, wait up. Wait up. I'm coming. I'm coming. Oh, that feels like it's close to 60. This is going to be one terrific blow-out. Mother Nature having a fit. Mom better fix tons of spaghetti. Everybody'll be there. Ooooh. Fun. I wonder who Uncle Rory'll drag in this time. Who the wind will blow into our lives. And out again. *(Exits.)*

Hanging Out

(Two friends, hanging out)

ASTRID: Here we are, in the middle of nowhere, doing absolutely nothing.

GRETCHEN: Aren't we lucky? Let's just lie here and look at the sky.

ASTRID: Make up cloud pictures.

GRETCHEN: That one's a dinosaur.

ASTRID: That one's a whale.

GRETCHEN: Or a walrus. See the tusks.

ASTRID: Now it's an elephant. The sky's a big kaleidoscope, isn't it? Always changing.

GRETCHEN: You got a doodle bug crawling up your arm.

ASTRID: That's a lucky sign.

GRETCHEN: They're cute, aren't they? *(Picks up doodle bug.)* Hello, little fella. You gonna bring us good luck today?

ASTRID: This is a lucky day. It's the first day we don't have to do anything. No school, volleyball, car wash, band practice, no nothing. A whole day to just hang out.

GRETCHEN: Think we can stand it?

ASTRID: I hope.

GRETCHEN: Maybe not the whole day.

ASTRID: Know what I wish?

GRETCHEN: You won the lottery.

ASTRID: That'd be good. No. I wish every day was like this. I don't mean with nothing to do. I couldn't stand that every day. But, I wish every day was different.

GRETCHEN: You mean, we didn't have to wake up at the same

time every day and be at school on time, and go to the same boring classes, and the same after school cheerleader practice and the same Friday night football game and tests every nine weeks? And baby-sitting Saturday nights.

ASTRID: You make it sound so regimented.

GRETCHEN: It is. But not today. Today, we've got nothing to do. Not one glorious thing.

ASTRID: What do you think would happen if people just did things when they wanted to?

GRETCHEN: Nothing would ever get done.

ASTRID: I don't believe that. I think more would be done, because people would want to do it.

GRETCHEN: Yes, but would it be the right things? I mean, who wants to pick up the garbage? Nobody, unless they have to. Or do homework on time?

ASTRID: If ever.

GRETCHEN: Maybe, if people did what they wanted when they wanted, maybe there wouldn't ever be any wars.

ASTRID: You think?

GRETCHEN: I don't know. I doubt it. Guys like to fight. But maybe there wouldn't be some other bad things ... like murder and robbery and stuff like that.

ASTRID: This discussion is getting too deep for me. Oh look. The dinosaur's turned into a monkey.

GRETCHEN: I'm so sleepy. Being outside always makes me sleepy.

ASTRID: It's probably the pollen.

GRETCHEN: *(Gives a big yawn. Curls up and falls asleep.)*

ASTRID: When I look up at the sky, I always think about all those planets out there, and stars. I mean, there must be other folks somewhere. Not like us, but creatures of some sort. Don't you think? Hey. You 'wake? Nope. Sound asleep. I guess I'll check out too. Got nothing else to do. *(Closes eyes and goes to sleep.)*

The Bestest Dog

CINDY: Please take him. Please. I'm beggin' you.

SHANNON: I'd like to help you but ...

CINDY: But you've got all that land. I'll buy his food. I'll come play with him every day. And bathe him every week. All you have to do is let him live at your place, till I can figure something out. It won't be long. I promise.

SHANNON: Can't you get your mom to let you keep him?

CINDY: She says he's just a bad dog. But that's not true. She just doesn't like him.

SHANNON: Well, Doodle does bark a lot. And chases people, and didn't he bite the UPS guy?

CINDY: But he's getting better.

SHANNON: He messes up a lot, doesn't he? I don't think my mom wants all that mess. I mean, I know some of the things he's done.

CINDY: That's because he was mad at my mom. He knows she doesn't like him. She should treat him better. It's her own fault.

SHANNON: Cindy, it's not your mom's fault the dog acts bad.

CINDY: Well, I'm going to move out anyway. As soon as I graduate. And I'll take him with me.

SHANNON: That's going to be pretty hard. Most people don't want to rent to people with dogs, do they?

CINDY: What am I going to do?

SHANNON: I don't know.

CINDY: What would you do if you were me?

SHANNON: I'd get rid of the dog. I mean, my mom's the most important person in my life. I wouldn't want a dog to come between us.

CINDY: But, he's my dog. I love him.

SHANNON: I wish I could help you. I really do. But, I know my mom won't let me bring him to our place. Sometimes, y'know, dogs really aren't very good. Maybe your mom's right.

CINDY: No, she isn't. Doodle's a good dog. He's a great dog. He's the bestest dog in the world.

SHANNON: I know you love him, but is he worth it? I mean, you and your mom fight a lot about the dog. He creates a lot of turmoil. My family likes peace and quiet and I just don't think he'd go with our lifestyle.

CINDY: Doodle's my dog and I'm not getting rid of him. I'll run away from home, if I have to, but I'm not giving him up no matter what she says.

SHANNON: Good luck. Let me know what happens. *(Exits.)*

CINDY: What am I going to do? I love my mom, and I love my dog. I don't see why I have to choose between them. Why can't I have both? Why does it have to be this way? Why do I have to make a choice?

Cyber Romance

CONNIE: You're what? You're doing what? Going where?

BRENDA: Not so loud. I don't want anyone to know. I'm only telling you because you're my best friend.

CONNIE: You've lost it, Brenda. This is going too far.

BRENDA: Thanks for the support, Connie. I thought I could count on you.

CONNIE: You can count on me to talk you out of it.

BRENDA: I don't want you to. I want to go. See. I have a ticket and everything. He sent it to me.

CONNIE: Nobody in their right mind goes off to a strange city where they know nobody, to meet some yahoo she met on the internet.

BRENDA: Of course I know him. We've been chatting for months now. You should talk to him. You'd like him.

CONNIE: And you've kept this secret from your parents, haven't you?

BRENDA: What do they care? They're so busy with their own lives, they'll never even know I'm gone.

CONNIE: Brenda, I'm telling you, this is insane.

BRENDA: It's an adventure. A romantic adventure.

CONNIE: More like a suicide mission. Look, I've read stories about women who meet these guys on the internet and the bad things that happen to them. One woman left her husband and kids and you know what, she got murdered.

BRENDA: Oh, that won't happen to me.

CONNIE: It could. And it might, if you go on this trip. This is dangerous.

BRENDA: I think we could have a life together, maybe even get married.

CONNIE: How old is he?

BRENDA: Twenty-four.

CONNIE: He's probably forty-five, maybe even fifty. What does he do?

BRENDA: Works for a stock broker company. He's very wealthy.

CONNIE: Probably a drug dealer. And married. And a pervert with some weird disease that he just can't wait to give you.

BRENDA: Connie, stop. You're such an alarmist. Really. Not all people on the internet are bad. I'm not.

CONNIE: Brenda! You just don't get it.

BRENDA: What?

CONNIE: Nothing.

BRENDA: Connie!

CONNIE: I never told anybody this, but, once, not that long ago either, I saw a man I thought was the hottest thing in pants. He was older, but that made him even more alluring. He looked sophisticated, and rich, and all those things we dream about. I followed him around piling on fantasy after fantasy about the life we'd live together. By the time I was through, this guy was Prince Charming, Leo, Brad, and whoever in one package. Then one night, I was out at the skating rink, and guess who was there? Drunk, and trying to pick up young girls. He even approached me. He smelled so awful I wanted to vomit. Now, ask yourself. If this guy's so terrific, why doesn't he come to your home, meet your folks, take you out on a proper date? Like real people. Regular, normal, nice people.

BRENDA: I told him I was twenty-two and a college student, and that I was going to be a doctor.

CONNIE: Great. He's got you lying too.

BRENDA: I didn't want him to know I'm only sixteen.

CONNIE: He knows. That's why he's taking advantage of you.

BRENDA: You really think so?

CONNIE: *(Takes ticket, tears it up.)* I'm going to get a hamburger. You hungry?

BRENDA: Hungry? I could eat a cow.

Mah-Jongg

P.K.: I wish you'd come with us. You know it's going to be great.

LILY: I always go to my grandmother's on Thursday nights.

P.K.: Can't you get out of it, just this once?

LILY: I don't want to. I love going to my grandmother's.

P.K.: You can see your grandma any time. This concert's one night only.

LILY: They'll have to concert without me. I'm playing Mah-Jongg.

P.K.: What's that? A new musical instrument?

LILY: It's a game. My grandmother and her friends and I play Mah-Jongg every Thursday night. We have, for months now.

P.K.: You're going to sit around with a bunch of old ladies when you could be at the concert? I don't believe it.

LILY: They're not old ladies. Well, they are old. But not old-old. They're lots of fun.

P.K.: I doubt it.

LILY: One's been married four times. She tells these incredible stories of all the adventures she's had, with all her husbands. She even lived in Saudi Arabia and had to wear a veil.

P.K.: Sounds thrilling.

LILY: Another one plays the stock market. She's offered to help me start building my portfolio. So, I can be rich, while I'm still young enough to enjoy it. Don't wait till you're old like me, she says.

P.K.: What a drag. Nobody understands all that stock market stuff.

LILY: She does. The other one likes to go fishing, so she's taking us all down to her camp on the river next weekend, so we can fish and play Mah-Jongg.

P.K.: Whoopee.

LILY: Aren't you glad she didn't invite you.

P.K.: So you're not going to the concert?

LILY: My grandmother's going to show us the plans for the new house she's building, out of straw. No, it isn't like the three little pigs. It's the latest in energy-saving houses. Keeps you cool in summer, warm in winter.

P.K.: Big deal. But, you should come with us. It's this great new rap group. They're so bad. You'll love it.

LILY: I can't think of anything less interesting than four hours with a bunch of egomaniacs prancing around on stage pretending to be rebellious when all they're really doing is getting rich off of people like you and me. Besides, they play so loud it hurts my ears.

P.K.: Sorry I asked. You sound like an old lady already.

LILY: Those old ladies are having more fun than you and me put together. They're totally awesome, and I want to be just like them, when I get old.

P.K.: Don't worry. You will.

LILY: Thanks for the compliment. Have fun. *(Exits.)*

P.K.: That girl has lost her mind. *(Exits.)*

Dick, Derek

CHAI: I don't know what to do. I can't go with both of them.

GRETA: We all should have your problem. Two terrific guys wanting to take you to the Harvest Dance.

CHAI: I really like Dick.

GRETA: Good. You should go with Dick.

CHAI: Maybe I should flip a coin. Heads Dick, tails Derek.

GRETA: Here's a quarter.

CHAI: But if Dick wins, everybody'll be mad at me. Derek's parents are my parents' best friends. Our Dads are always doing things together and his mom and mine are like sisters.

GRETA: Then you should go with Dick. Going with Derek'll be like going with your brother.

CHAI: Mom says I'll have to choose, and she's sure I'll make the right choice.

GRETA: What does that mean?

CHAI: I don't know. I better read my horoscope, and see what it says. Maybe this isn't a good day to make a decision.

GRETA: Derek's a real prize. I've always wanted to date him.

CHAI: Really? Why? I've always thought him a little strange.

GRETA: That's why he's so cool. All that Egyptology and hieroglyphics and pyramid lore. I love it.

CHAI: He is different. Dick's more normal. So, you think I should go with Derek.

GRETA: Have you heard anything I've said?

CHAI: But I don't know what to do. Have you got some Tarot Cards? I should do a reading.

GRETA: You should follow your heart and go with whoever you

want to, no matter what your parents or anybody else says. Your heart will lead you down the pathway to romance. Isn't that poetic?

CHAI: You make it sound like walking down the aisle. I just want to have a good time at the dance. I know. Let's go catch some beetles.

GRETA: No thanks. I'm not hungry.

CHAI: We'll put them in a circle. Put some red fingernail polish on one of them. That can be Dick. Or Derek. It doesn't matter. They have to get out of the circle. First one out, that's who I go with.

GRETA: Why don't you just go with who you want? Make your own decision.

CHAI: 'Cause I don't know who I want to go with.

GRETA: If you could go with anybody in the world, no matter what anybody said, who would it be?

CHAI: Arnold.

GRETA: Arnold? Where'd he come from?

CHAI: Oh, this is hopeless.

GRETA: Did Arnold ask you?

CHAI: No. But I wish he would.

GRETA: You can fix that, easy.

CHAI: I can? How?

GRETA: Now you're making me crazy.

CHAI: Do you think I should go with Arnold?

GRETA: I think I'm going bowling.

CHAI: But wait. You have to help me make up my mind.

GRETA: Forget it. That's not possible. *(Exits.)*

CHAI: I know. I'll get a daisy. I'll pull the petals...Derek, Dick. Derek. Dick. Derek, Dick. Arnold. Derek, Dick, Arnold. Arnold, Dick, Derek.

Helping Out

TRACY: I don't understand algebra, do you?

MEG: I'm working on it. *(Phone rings. TRACY answers. MEG studies.)*

TRACY: Hello. *(Pause)* Yes. *(Pause)* Jamestown. The founding of Jamestown. *(Pause)* How long? *(Pause)* Five pages. And it has to be printed out on the computer. *(Pause)* Yes. *(Pause)* No. *(Pause)* It's not a problem. I can do it. It's due Monday. *(Pause)* OK. *(Pause)* Sure. Goodbye.

MEG: What was that all about?

TRACY: That was Mrs. Cooper.

MEG: Roy's mom? What did she want?

TRACY: She wants me to write a paper he has to have for American History.

MEG: You didn't tell her yes, did you? You did, didn't you?

TRACY: What else could I say?

MEG: You say no. I can't believe Roy's mother is calling you to do his homework. Do you even know her?

TRACY: She and my mom work together. She doesn't have time to do it, because she has to work this weekend. They have a big meeting.

MEG: Roy's mom does all his homework! Now she wants you to. Really.

TRACY: Roy's my friend. Aren't we supposed to help our friends when they need it?

MEG: I don't see how doing someone's homework is helping them out. It's just setting them up to fail.

TRACY: And there's the big game in three weeks.

MEG: Oh. The big game. And of course, everything depends on Roy, right?

TRACY: He is the best player on the team. It'll be terrible if we lose. And besides, I don't mind helping out.

MEG: Tracy. Suppose ... now just suppose ... that ten or fifteen years from now, Roy has a job and his boss needs him to do something really important. His whole job depends on it. Are you going to be there to help him? Is his mom going to be there? Bad question. She probably will.

TRACY: That's silly. Of course I won't be there. And neither will she.

MEG: That's why you can't write his paper. He has to learn to do his own work. Or where will he ever get in life?

TRACY: But I told his mom I'd help.

MEG: You can un-tell her. The world won't come to an end.

TRACY: What do I say?

MEG: The truth. You're really doing him a favor. I can't even believe she asked you. That's too bizarre.

TRACY: I just hate to get her mad at me. And my mom. You don't think she'll take it out on my mom, at work? Maybe sabotage her or something.

MEG: Knowing your mom, I think she can handle it.

TRACY: I know you're right. But ...

MEG: It's pretty hard to say no to adults. She's taking advantage of you.

TRACY: I better call her. *(Picks up phone, dials.)* Hello. Mrs. Cooper. This is Tracy. *(Pause)* Look, on that paper you called about. I'm not going to be able to do it. *(Pause)* No. I just don't feel right about it. *(Pause)* I'm sorry you feel that way. Goodbye.

MEG: She got mad didn't she?

TRACY: I hope she doesn't do anything to hurt my mom. So. Where were we ... Algebra. I hope some day I understand this stuff.

True Love

BABS: Hey, Lizette. Wait up.

LIZETTE: *(Ignores her.)*

BABS: Didn't you hear me?

LIZETTE: Oh. Hi.

BABS: Are you alive?

LIZETTE: What? Oh. Yeah. *(Cell phone rings.)* Hello. *(Pause)* Oh. Hello, Bob. *(Pause)* OK. *(Pause)* I already have a date. *(Pause)* Bye. *(Hangs up.)*

BABS: So, we gonna study tonight? For the Big Test.

LIZETTE: We have a test?

BABS: You know, the Big Test. Lizette, what's with you?

LIZETTE: What?

BABS: Who is it this time?

LIZETTE: What?

BABS: Who are you in love with today?

LIZETTE: Whatever.

BABS: You're always in love. A different guy every week.

LIZETTE: *(Phone rings.)* Hello. *(Pause)* Oh. Roger. It's you. I told you not to call me anymore. *(Pause)* No. I don't want to talk to you. *(Pause)* No. *(Hangs up.)*

BABS: You've already been through James, Christian, Jay, Yost, Luis and Tiger, Roger and Bob, so it has to be either Lee, Manuel, or Tyrone.

LIZETTE: Nope. None of the above. Besides those were just boys. Only worthy of my passing fancy.

BABS: If we don't study tonight, we won't be passing anything, fancy or not. If it's not Lee, Manuel, or Tyrone, who is it?

LIZETTE: Nobody you know.

BABS: Oh no. Now you're recruiting from the outfield. You really are in trouble.

LIZETTE: Trouble like this should come along every day.

BABS: Right. Here today, gone tomorrow. I know you.

LIZETTE: Wrong. This is true love.

BABS: When'd you meet him?

LIZETTE: At the debate conference.

BABS: Nobody finds true love at the debate conference.

LIZETTE: Oh. Where do you find it? In a bar?

BABS: Where else? What's his name? Is it Gregory? But I can't imagine him at a debate tournament.

LIZETTE: Gregory. What makes you think I could ever like him?

BABS: He's the one person you've talked about since forever. So. If it's not Gregory, who is it?

LIZETTE: Kim. Kim Li.

BABS: Kim Lee who?

LIZETTE: Kim Li. That's his name.

BABS: Nobody's named Kim Lee. Oh. Kim Li. Gotcha.

LIZETTE: Oh, Babs. He's so wonderful. He's brilliant. Gorgeous. Funny. You should have heard him debate. He's a genius.

BABS: So was Luis. And James. Ditto Yost. Yadda yadda yadda.

LIZETTE: Oh, go away. Just because you never have any boyfriends, you want to spoil it for the rest of us. Anyway, I intend to marry him.

BABS: Like you were going to marry Luis, and everybody else on the planet.

LIZETTE: This time's different. It's time for me to stop playing the field and settle down. Get into a real relationship.

BABS: Yes. It is. This time, it really is true love.

LIZETTE: *(Cell phone rings.)* Hello. *(Pause)* Oh. Hi. *(Pause)* Nothing. Talking to Babs. *(Pause)* No. *(Pause)* Oh. This is a surprise. *(Pause)* No. No. *(Pause)* No. *(Pause)* Yes. *(Pause)* Yes. *(Pause)* Yes. I'd love to. *(Pause)* OK. Bye. See you Saturday. *(Hangs up.)*

BABS: Kim Li?

LIZETTE: Gregory. He wants to take me to the big game Saturday night.

BABS: I guess you and Kim Li won't be eloping this weekend.

LIZETTE: Eloping? Good grief. I'm too young for all that. So, what time you want to get together tonight? I'll be so glad when the Big Test is over.

BABS: Know something, Lizzie? I don't think it ever is. I think there's always a Big Test out there somewhere, lurking in the bushes, waiting to pounce.

LIZETTE: Oh, that's too depressing to even think about. Now, let's see. What shall I wear? I'll buy myself a new sweater. A pink angora sweater. Guys love fuzzy stuff. And dangly earrings. And I look too great in pink.

New York, New York

MAGGIE: I hope you're ready to go out. Because we've already wasted half the morning while you fiddle around.

T.K.: Wait a minute. I have to hide my purse. *(Pulls coat over purse.)*

MAGGIE: You look stupid. And you can't move your arms.

T.K.: You know everybody in New York gets their purse snatched.

MAGGIE: I don't think so. So. This is the plan. We'll take the subway to ...

T.K.: No. We can't take the subway. We'll get mugged.

MAGGIE: We'll take a taxi.

T.K.: No. They'll kidnap us.

MAGGIE: Nobody's going to kidnap us. But all right. We'll go on the bus.

T.K.: We'll get all lost and confused, changing buses. We'll end up in some terrible place where we'll be knifed and murdered and nobody will ever find our bodies.

MAGGIE: All right. How are we going to go to the Museum? Walk?

T.K.: No. It's too dangerous. All those homeless people, waiting to attack us. They're all crazy.

MAGGIE: T.K., tell me how we got here.

T.K.: Your dad came on a business trip and you invited me to come. Why?

MAGGIE: So I can have it indelibly imbedded in my brain never to be forgotten and never ever again to be duplicated. You've done nothing since we got here except exhibit paranoid tendencies that border on the insane. You think everybody's out to get you.

T.K.: Aren't they?

MAGGIE: You thought the taxi driver last night was some kind of lunatic, and the man who brought up our luggage was staring at you. Why did you come if you're afraid of everything and everybody?

T.K.: I wanted to see New York.

MAGGIE: So. Let's go see it.

T.K.: You're right. I am being stupid.

MAGGIE: Now then. This is the plan. We'll take the bus to the Museum.

T.K.: But we can't talk to anybody.

MAGGIE: I don't think many muggers hang out at the Metropolitan Museum of Art.

T.K.: And no weird food.

MAGGIE: T.K., I think you should seriously consider taking the next plane back home. I don't think you're ready for New York.

T.K.: No, no. I'll be fine. Really. It's just that all my life I've heard stories about how dangerous New York is.

MAGGIE: I was here last spring and went everywhere without any problem. You just have to be careful. We're not going into any bad places. Look. I was born in a little tiny town in the country. Then we moved to a big town. I heard my folks talking about all the bad things that could happen. I was terrified. I never wanted to leave the house. Then one day, I realized that I couldn't live my whole life in fear. 'Cause if I did, I wouldn't have much of a life. Now, I'm going to the Museum. I'm going to talk to people. And eat in a deli. The wilder the food, the better. I'll probably go to a movie too, which probably isn't even in English.

T.K.: You don't have to be so ugly.

MAGGIE: You don't have to be so obnoxious.

T.K.: You're really insensitive, aren't you?

MAGGIE: I'm leaving. I'm going to the Museum to look at the statues.

T.K.: That's right. Leave me here by myself.

MAGGIE: T.K. You're my guest, but that doesn't mean I'll let you ruin my trip. Now, are you coming, or not? Tell you what, come with me, and if you don't like it, if you're totally miserable, I'll put you in a taxi to the airport. How's that?

T.K.: Fine.

MAGGIE: Do you want to take your suitcase? Just in case.

T.K.: No.

MAGGIE: You sure?

T.K.: I'm sure.

MAGGIE: Fine.

T.K.: Maggie. Thanks for inviting me to come with you. You could have asked a lot of people, but you didn't. I won't ruin your trip. I'll get over it.

MAGGIE: I know. C'mon. Let's get out of here. *(Both exit.)*

Matchmakers

KIEMA: You're so lucky, going to live on an island for a month. Just you and your grandmother.

MARILYN: And you're going to see your grandfather in Wisconsin.

KIEMA: I can hardly wait. I always have the best time in the world at Grandpa's. He lives out by this gorgeous lake. It's a summer resort area, so there's lots of kids. I've got lots of summer friends there.

MARILYN: Any interesting guys?

KIEMA: A few.

MARILYN: I'm excited too, about the island. It's off one of the Florida keys. You can only get there by boat. Grandma's friend has a camp she's letting us use. And you know what? We aren't taking any food. Grandma says we're going to fish for everything and live off the land.

KIEMA: You'll starve to death. No cokes or anything? No pizza? How will you stand it?

MARILYN: Don't worry. Grandma loves ice cream, and I don't think she'll last a week. But, she has this idea I should know what it's like to live in a primitive culture.

KIEMA: Why? Why should anybody live in a primitive culture?

MARILYN: She's like that. She has rather wild ideas about things sometimes. Like when grandpa died, she painted her face like an Indian.

KIEMA: Neat. I bet she looked great.

MARILYN: I thought so. But Mom worried that she'd lost her mind.

KIEMA: Did she?

MARILYN: I don't think so. She was just grieving. But she went out west and lived with the Indians for a while. I visited her and met the medicine man and the chief. Went to a sweat lodge and all the dances.

KIEMA: Fun. My grandpa's the sheriff. He takes me riding in his sheriff's car with the lights blinking. It's kind of exciting.

MARILYN: Do you meet all the criminals?

KIEMA: It's pretty peaceful up at the lake. No Colombian drug dealers or serial killers. No gangs. They fish a lot, and go to bed early.

MARILYN: Know what I like best about my grammy? She's kind of old. I mean, she is old. But she's always trying out new ideas and thinking up fun things to do. Last year she took me to Mexico, to this world peace conference. I met people from all over the world. She knows everybody. Even some African chief, who gave me a lion's tooth necklace.

KIEMA: Grandpa's like that too. He knows everybody up at the lake. And he's a real hero. He's saved all kinds of people who wrecked their boats, or got lost in the woods, or hurt themselves hiking. Next to my dad, he's the neatest guy in the world. He's been pretty lonely, since Grandma died. Think we could get them together?

MARILYN: She's coming back home with me, after our month on the island.

KIEMA: Bet I can convince Grandpa to come home with me. What do you think?

MARILYN: But we can't tell them. They have to meet, casual like.

KIEMA: Oh, this is going to be a great summer.

CHIQUITA: We should go this way.
MARGUERITE: No, this way.
CHIQUITA: No. This way.
MARGUERITE: No. This way.
CHIQUITA: No.
MARGUERITE: This way?
CHIQUITA: We're lost.
MARGUERITE: I don't think so. I think it's over here. But I'm not sure.
CHIQUITA: I'm all turned upside down and backwards. I don't even know how we got here.
MARGUERITE: We came from over here.
CHIQUITA: No. We came from here.
MARGUERITE: Maybe it was over here.
CHIQUITA: Or here. Or here. Or here.
MARGUERITE: But, how do we get out?
CHIQUITA: It is a puzzle. We might as well sit down and wait.
MARGUERITE: For what? Who's coming to help us? Nobody I know.
CHIQUITA: We have to get ourselves un-confused.
MARGUERITE: I am pretty befuddled.
CHIQUITA: We're lost. A few moments ago, we were on our merry way, and now, look at us.
MARGUERITE: It's very baffling.
TOGETHER: We're lost.
CHIQUITA: We simply have to wait.
MARGUERITE: Till ... ?
CHIQUITA: Shhhhh.
MARGUERITE: You hear something?

CHIQUITA: No. I thought so, but, no. Whatever it was, is gone.
MARGUERITE: Think we're in any danger?
CHIQUITA: Hmmmm. Perhaps. Probably not. But, you never know.
MARGUERITE: Could this be a mystical moment?
CHIQUITA: Shhhhh. Hear that?
MARGUERITE: I do. What is it?
CHIQUITA: Who knows?
MARGUERITE: There it is again.
CHIQUITA: It's the sound of the future calling. Luring us into its web of infinite possibilities.
MARGUERITE: It's stopped. Does that mean we're stuck in the present?
CHIQUITA: Perhaps the past. *(Lies down, as if to sleep.)*
MARGUERITE: What are you doing? You can't go to sleep now.
CHIQUITA: What else have we to do? Unless you have a plan. Have you?
MARGUERITE: Go to sleep if you want. I'll wake you if something happens.
CHIQUITA: You'll man the first watch, won't you?
MARGUERITE: What shall I watch for?
CHIQUITA: A way out.
MARGUERITE: I suppose there'll be a sign. This way out. With a big arrow pointing.
CHIQUITA: Probably.
MARGUERITE: Sweet dreams.
CHIQUITA: Sweet watch.
MARGUERITE: There's that sound again. Hear it?
CHIQUITA: Shhhh. I'm dreaming.
MARGUERITE: Dream us out of here, please. *(Long pause.)*
CHIQUITA: Are we still here?
MARGUERITE: We're still lost.
CHIQUITA: We aren't lost.
MARGUERITE: We aren't?
CHIQUITA: We're here.
MARGUERITE: You're being very cryptic.
CHIQUITA: Oh. Do you see that sign, over there?
MARGUERITE: There's no sign. Where are you going?

CHIQUITA: I'm following the sign. This Way Out.

MARGUERITE: There's no sign.

CHIQUITA: Just follow me.

MARGUERITE: Following you got us here. No telling where you'll take us now.

CHIQUITA: This wasn't a bad place, was it?

MARGUERITE: I've been in better.

CHIQUITA: Are you coming?

MARGUERITE: No. I'll wait.

CHIQUITA: See you. *(Exits.)*

MARGUERITE: There's that sound again. I wonder what it is. I wonder if I'll ever know. It sounds like, like a distant roar, maybe thunder, maybe rain. Maybe a baby crying, or perhaps a cow. It isn't calling, it's just there. Sometimes I hear it over here, sometimes over here. Sometimes right here, in the center of things. Perhaps it is my heart. Or my fear. Maybe my hope. I'll just sit and wait. Wait till ... there. Over there. I see it. I see the sign. But it isn't the same ... no. Of course. It wouldn't be. Follow the sign. That's all I can do. Follow the sign. This way out. *(Exits, opposite.)*

Friends Again

MALAIKA: So, Sabrina. I heard your house got wrapped with toilet paper last night. I bet that was a thrill.

SABRINA: You wouldn't know anything about it, would you? You and all the other cheerleaders?

MALAIKA: Why should we? We were at the big game. And where were you? Too afraid to show your face, now that Johnny's not your main man anymore?

SABRINA: You know all the news, don't you?

MALAIKA: That you dumped him, just before the game. How could you? You broke his heart. He was so depressed he hardly scored. That's why we lost. To our arch rivals. And it's all your fault.

SABRINA: I'm glad you think I'm so powerful that I could lose a game I didn't even attend. Thanks for the compliment.

MALAIKA: How could you dump him? He's the coolest guy in town.

SABRINA: He's all yours now, if you want him.

MALAIKA: What do you mean? Why wouldn't I want him? Who wouldn't? He's totally gorgeous.

SABRINA: He's totally boring.

MALAIKA: Boring? No way. All you have to do is look at that awesome face and lights start popping.

SABRINA: Take him. From what I see, you two probably deserve each other.

MALAIKA: You got what you deserved. I just wish we'd done it sooner.

SABRINA: So, you and the cheerleaders did wrap my house. But why? We used to be friends. At least, I thought we were. Till you got to be a cheerleader. Since then everything's changed.

MALAIKA: You changed. You thought you were too good for the

rest of us. You were above it all.

SABRINA: Why would you think that? You got in with that crowd, and all of a sudden you stopped being my friend.

MALAIKA: I thought it was the other way round.

SABRINA: I wish we could be friends again. I miss you. I miss the talks we used to have, and the way we'd do make up and clothes and learn the new dances. I thought we'd be friends forever. But, I guess I was wrong.

MALAIKA: It's too late for that now.

SABRINA: Why? Why is it too late? All we have to do is decide that's what we want. To be friends again. Know why I didn't try out for cheerleading?

MALAIKA: You thought you were better than the rest of us.

SABRINA: I thought I wouldn't make it. You and all the other girls were so good, I thought I didn't have a chance.

MALAIKA: That's dumb. You were the best.

SABRINA: You were.

MALAIKA: And Johnny. You think you're not good enough for him?

SABRINA: He's really a bore. He's a pretty face, yes, but empty mind. He's fine in a crowd, but get him alone, and it's really a drag. All he talks about is himself. The guy's a cliche.

MALAIKA: You really thought you weren't good enough for cheerleading?

SABRINA: Sad to say, I did. And I do.

MALAIKA: You want to be a cheerleader?

SABRINA: Sure. Who wouldn't?

MALAIKA: There might be a spot. Latoya's moving away.

SABRINA: You think I'd have a chance?

MALAIKA: I could work with you. Teach you some moves.

SABRINA: Would you? Thanks.

MALAIKA: Look. I'm really sorry about wrapping your house. We were so mad about losing the game, we had to take it out on somebody. I'll get the gang together and we'll come take it down.

SABRINA: My parent's are not happy. My dad called the principal this morning. He wants everybody who did it to be suspended.

MALAIKA: We better get over there. But it sure was fun doing it. I've never done anything like that before. It felt so wicked, you know? Daring.

SABRINA: When do you want to work on the cheers?

MALAIKA: Right now. Now. You have to remember to make big movements. Like this. *(Exit.)*

The Last Kiss of Summer

CYD: *(Polishing toenails)* This is the last time we'll ever see them again. Our last date in the whole world, forever and ever.

ANNIE: We don't know that.

CYD: You know how summer romances go. Here today ...

ANNIE: Gone tomorrow.

CYD: You both say you'll write.

ANNIE: But neither of you does.

CYD: You each simply disappear.

ANNIE: Back into your dull, dreary life back home.

CYD: Gone from each other's lives, forever.

ANNIE: One last kiss of summer, then poof, you're gone, vanished, into the mist.

CYD: Oh, that's too romantic. True love, lost in the mists of life.

ANNIE: If it's true love, nothing can keep you apart, so I've always heard.

CYD: But people are ripped apart, just when they find each other.

ANNIE: Like that Longfellow poem we read. Evangeline. Separated in youth, reunited finally after a lifetime of grief and sorrow.

CYD: It's so sad. But they did finally find each other, so maybe what you say is right. True love will not be denied.

ANNIE: Right. When they're so old they can barely stumble into each other's arms. What's the point?

CYD: They can die together, in each other's arms. What can be more romantic than that?

ANNIE: Living together. Building a life. A life of unrequited love seems like a big waste of time if you ask me.

CYD: Are you in love with Bud?

ANNIE: I doubt it. Are you in love with Bill?

CYD: Maybe. A little. A wee tiny bit. It's probably better this way. To know there's someone out there, wandering the earth, searching for your smile.

ANNIE: Looking for you behind every unopened door.

CYD: Walking down every rainswept street.

ANNIE: In every tucked-away café.

CYD: At the top of the Eiffel Tower.

ANNIE: At the post office.

CYD: In the burial chamber of the Great Pyramid.

ANNIE: That sounds like a bad case of fanny fatigue from riding some dirty old flea-bitten camel.

CYD: So. Do I look memorable, or don't I?

ANNIE: I hope I look utterly forgettable.

CYD: What?

ANNIE: So Bud can remember me simply as the wind.

CYD: Oh, how poetic. We're the gentle breeze that gusted into their lives that glorious summer at the beach.

ANNIE: Forever lingering.

CYD: Tingling into eternity.

ANNIE: Upon their sunburned skin.

CYD: Oh, rats. You made me get polish all over my toes. Why'd you do that?

ANNIE: Moi? Moi? Would I do that?

CYD: Get some on you, too. Take that. And that and that. *(Jabs her with fingernail polish brush.)*

ANNIE: Stop. Stop it, Cyd. No! You'll ruin my big date.

CYD: Why, Annie, you're really upset.

ANNIE: Hardly. Over a summer romance?

CYD: I thought you were being caustic because you didn't care. But you do, don't you? You really like this guy.

ANNIE: It's just a summer fling. A day at the beach, that's all.

CYD: Sure. Just another day at the beach.

ANNIE: It doesn't seem fair. To meet someone you really, really, really like. Who's everything you've ever looked for in a guy, and then he goes away and you never see him again.

CYD: You said it best, Annie.

ANNIE: What?

CYD: If it's true love, nothing can keep you apart.

ANNIE: I said that?

CYD: Now, where shall we go on this last night of summer vacation? To the beach, of course. Lying about on blankets on the sand, listening to the sound of the waves, looking up at the stars ...

ANNIE: Oh, Cyd, stop. Stop already. Get real. Get down to earth.

CYD: Why? We get down to earth every day of our lives. When we go back home, we'll have to get ready for school, then it'll be nothing but homework, tests, baby-sitting, boring ball games, dull dates. The most exciting thing in my life is ... nothing. I'm having a summer romance and I'm going to enjoy every precious, unreal, fantastical, romantical moment. Ooooh. I think that's their car. Ready?

ANNIE: No. Yes. No. I guess. Help!

CYD: Oh, this is going to be so great. The moon, the waves, the stars ...

ANNIE: You're driving me crazy with this stupid romantic stuff.

CYD: Maybe you should try it. It might improve your outlook on life. Everything doesn't have to always be grim and depressing, you know. And so what if you never see Bud again. You'll always know you had a great time this summer at the beach. You'll have memories. And all those pictures we took, out in the boat.

ANNIE: Yeah. Me tangled up in the sail and you throwing up over the side.

CYD: OK. Now, are you ready?

ANNIE: I'm ready. How do I look?

CYD: Memorable. Absolutely memorable.

ANNIE: Cyd.

CYD: Yes?

ANNIE: I hate you.

CYD: Good. Let's go. The last kiss of summer. Ah. Can we stand it?

Trios

Betraying the Blues

(ALL sitting around, reading fashion magazines. ALL are very stylish, in their own way. YVETTE sings softly.)

PAJ: Look at this.

YVETTE: It would look great on a skunk. Or a shark. Maybe even a vampire.

PAJ: I like it.

ORIANNA: Too retro.

YVETTE: This one has style.

PAJ: You leave your taste at the dump?

ORIANNA: What's with you two?

PAJ: Nothing.

YVETTE: Nothing.

ORIANNA: Yeah, yeah, yeah. I know a smoldering burn when I see it. When I feel it. You two are about to go off like firecrackers.

YVETTE: I don't know what you're talking about.

PAJ: Me either.

ORIANNA: OK. *(ALL read.)*

YVETTE: Now this is a great outfit.

ORIANNA: It's OK. Better than most. Still, it's kinda dumpy.

PAJ: Pity that poor model, getting stuck with that bit of fashion desperation.

YVETTE: It'd look terrific on you, Paj. Bring out your flair for the dramatic.

PAJ: My flair for the dramatic.

YVETTE: Yes. Think how much fun you'd have shocking everyone.

PAJ: Me shocking everyone.

YVETTE: It'd be great for your big betrayal scene.

ORIANNA: Look you two. What is going on? Let's get it out.
YVETTE: Nothing's going on. *(ALL read.)*
ORIANNA: This one's it.
PAJ: That?
YVETTE: I love it.
PAJ: Not on this body.
YVETTE: You becoming a fashion snob?
PAJ: Those clothes belong in a toxic dump.
ORIANNA: Look. You two better tell me what's going on, or I am out of here.
PAJ: Nothing's going on.
YVETTE: She just ...
PAJ: What? I just what ...
YVETTE: I don't want to talk about it.
ORIANNA: You need to talk about it.
YVETTE: No, I don't.
ORIANNA: Yes, you do. Talking about it makes it go away. Makes you feel better. Whenever I have troubles, I always talk about it. Get it out of my system. So. What's this all about?
PAJ: I really don't know.
YVETTE: Yes you do.
PAJ: I don't.
YVETTE: That's just like you.
ORIANNA: I'm leaving.
YVETTE: You know, the other night, when we were all going to the dance. And Paj was late.
PAJ: I told you. My mom didn't get home. I couldn't leave my little brother alone.
YVETTE: A convenient excuse.
PAJ: Don't believe me then.
ORIANNA: I don't even know what you're talking about. I was late too.
YVETTE: But you didn't lie about it.
PAJ: I didn't lie. My mother was late.
YVETTE: That part may be true. But you also went to the ...
PAJ: Oh. That's what you're mad about.
YVETTE: Wouldn't you be, too?
ORIANNA: What are you talking about?!

PAJ: Instead of going straight to the dance, I went to the ...
YVETTE: She went, without us.
ORIANNA: Where?
YVETTE: We always said we'd go together. The three of us.
ORIANNA: Without us. You went without us.
PAJ: It was just a spur of the moment thing. I didn't plan it.
ORIANNA: So what happened?
PAJ: He was very professional. He asked me to come back when his partner was there.
ORIANNA: Who's his partner?
PAJ: His sister. They're twins. He does the photography, she does the bookings. He wants her to meet me.
ORIANNA: You went without us. How could you do that?
PAJ: Because, you two are always talking about doing things, but you never do 'em.
YVETTE: I feel so betrayed.
ORIANNA: You went without us. You betrayed us.
PAJ: You can feel that way. Or you can be happy for me. It's your choice.
YVETTE: Maybe I'll be happy for you next week. But not today. Maybe never.
ORIANNA: I'm jealous. And proud. At least you did it. When do you meet the sister?
PAJ: Tomorrow.
ORIANNA: Why didn't you tell us, Paj?
PAJ: I knew you'd get mad.
ORIANNA: We were going to do it all together.
PAJ: Every time we planned it, something always came up. Your hair wasn't right, or your nails weren't perfect, or your toes weren't painted. I was tired of excuses. So, when I walked past his place, I just went for it.
YVETTE: Do you think you could get him to see me?
PAJ: He'll see you, but you don't need me.
YVETTE: So you won't help a friend now that you're a big model.
PAJ: I'm not a big model. But I think sometimes you do better on your own.
ORIANNA: You just walked in, without an appointment.

PAJ: He was fiddling around with the lights. It was cool.
YVETTE: I'm going. Right now.
PAJ: Good for you. Go for it. Orianna?
YVETTE: Come with me. We can go together.
ORIANNA: I'm not ready.
YVETTE: 'Course you are. I'll be with you. You don't have to be afraid.
ORIANNA: I'm not afraid. I'm just not ready.
PAJ: You're never going to be ready, are you?
ORIANNA: I guess not.
YVETTE: What? Why not? C'mon. This is our big chance. He's already taken Paj. He'll take us, too.
ORIANNA: I don't really want to be a model.
YVETTE: We've all wanted to be models since we were ... well, since forever.
ORIANNA: I want to go live in the woods and be a biologist or something. I like animals.
PAJ: You'll be the most stylish mountain woman out there tromping them woods, feeding them wolves, fighting them thare bears.
ORIANNA: I guess, now that you've done it, Paj, I don't have to. You didn't really betray me, y'know. You liberated me.
YVETTE: I never really wanted to be a model. I just always thought if I was a model first, that would help my singing career.
PAJ: Good grief, girl.
YVETTE: I didn't want to disappoint you two. We always said we'd stick together. I didn't want to betray the group.
PAJ: Get out there and sing. It's what you really want.
YVETTE: It's what I've always wanted.
ORIANNA: We're liberated now, gal. Liberated. Free to do our own thing. Wow! What a great feeling. I was trying to think of a way to tell y'all I didn't want to be a glamour queen, and now I don't have to.
YVETTE: Now that's a great dress for any diva. *(Starts to sing.)*
PAJ and ORIANNA: Sing it, gal. Sing it.

(YVETTE sings in full voice. PAJ and ORIANNA clap in time, then join in, singing backup. At song's end, they all hug, laughing and dancing around the stage. A joyful moment, of friends, sharing hopes, dreams, and themselves.)

When We Grow Up

(Three girls, chatting. CYRA fixes VERNIQUE's hair. NAKIA browses through a book.)

NAKIA: Anybody write their essay yet?

VERNIQUE: Which one?

CYRA: I did the one on Freedom of Speech for Mr. Jackson.

NAKIA: The one on Career Choices, for Mrs. Lovett.

CYRA: I started, but didn't get very far. I don't know what I want to be.

VERNIQUE: I know what I want to be.

CYRA: An actress.

VERNIQUE: No. A postman.

NAKIA: They're called letter carriers.

VERNIQUE: OK. I want to be a letter carrier.

CYRA: Talk about boring. Walking around all day being chased by dogs.

VERNIQUE: My neighbor's a postman.

NAKIA: Letter carrier.

VERNIQUE: Whatever. He has a very nice life. And a beautiful garden. I love his garden. He has the most gorgeous flowers you ever saw.

NAKIA: There's nothing I don't want to be. Nothing I don't want to know. I love to draw and dance, and sing, and play the guitar. I just wish I could do it all at the same time. I want to be one of everything.

VERNIQUE: Like garbage collector? Somebody's maid? How 'bout prison guard?

CYRA: Or coal miner? I know. You could be the person who cleans up after the dogs at the dog pound.

NAKIA: Why are y'all being so mean to me?

VERNIQUE: 'Cause you sound so dumb. Be everything. Do everything. Nobody can do that.

NAKIA: Best have too many choices, than none, like you, Cyra. You can't think of anything?

CYRA: I like doing hair.

VERNIQUE: You'd do good, being a hair dresser.

CYRA: Cosmetologist. My cousin's at cosmetology school. He loves it.

VERNIQUE: My grandmother wants me to go to college.

NAKIA: I'll have to get some kinda scholarship, or I can't go.

VERNIQUE: All that studying. Writing papers and reports. I can't think of anything worse.

CYRA: Me neither.

NAKIA: I want to learn everything. Maybe that can be my career. Learning.

CYRA: Boring.

VERNIQUE: Hard. Too hard for me. I'll be a postman.

NAKIA: Vernique, do you think being a letter carrier'll get you a beautiful garden?

VERNIQUE: Mr. Seaberry lets me help him weed and water his plants. He showed me how to plant the seeds in little cups, then move 'em when they've grown up a bit. He knows everything about plants.

NAKIA: Why don't you just be a horticulturist?

VERNIQUE: What's that?

NAKIA: A gardener, with a big fancy name.

CYRA: I want my own salon one day. My cousin say he knows a lady who makes twenty-five thousand dollars a year.

VERNIQUE: That's a lotta money.

NAKIA: Maybe I should forget college, and start cutting hair.

VERNIQUE: Oh, you're too smart, Nakia. You should be like a professor or something.

CYRA: You're always reading those books. I bet you end up writing 'em.

NAKIA: I write stories at night, before I fall asleep.

CYRA: See, you're already a author.

VERNIQUE: Authoress. Mrs. Lovett said women writers are called authoresses.

NAKIA: Me. An authoress. I can do that. Authoress. Writing stories all my life. What could be better than that?

VERNIQUE: Oh. I'm sure you'll think of something. Probably two or three.

Quartets

Scream

(EMMA on stage, screaming. Practicing screaming. Not especially loud, but certainly expressive. High pitched screams and low wild screams. Controlled. Screams that come like puffs of smoke. Screams that roll like thunder. DEBRA enters.)

DEBRA: Think you're getting it.

EMMA: Hard to tell. How's this? *(Screams.)*

DEBRA: Getting better.

EMMA: I like this one. *(Screams.)*

DEBRA: Hey. I like that too. Do it again.

EMMA: *(Repeats scream, with variation.)*

DEBRA: I think you got it.

EMMA: It's getting close.

DEBRA: Keep trying. You'll get there. *(Exits.)*

EMMA: *(Practices screaming. Much body language and movement.)*

YOKO: *(Enters.)* Hi, Emma. How's the screaming going?

EMMA: *(Loud scream)*

YOKO: All right! Mind if I try? *(Screams.)*

EMMA: We sound pretty good together, don't we?

LATOYA: *(Enters.)* What are you two doing?

EMMA and YOKO: *(Scream.)*

LATOYA: I got that. But what are you doing?

EMMA and YOKO: *(Scream.)*

LATOYA: OK. I get it. This is some kind of joke, right?

EMMA: It's no joke.

YOKO: She's very good, don't you think?

LATOYA: Great. If you like screaming. Doesn't it hurt your voice?

EMMA: It comes from your stomach, not your throat. Actually, it's pretty easy.

LATOYA: Whatever.
EMMA: This way, you can scream all day. *(Screams.)*
YOKO: C'mon Latoya. Give it a shot.
LATOYA: I'd rather not.
YOKO: Coward.
LATOYA: I just don't think screaming is a very worthwhile pursuit.
EMMA: Oh, but you're wrong. It's very worthwhile.
LATOYA: I don't get it.
EMMA: You know how it is. You never figure anything out till you actually do it.
LATOYA: OK. I'll try. *(Screams.)*
EMMA: Pretty good, actually. For your first time.
LATOYA: But I still don't get it.
EMMA: Try it again.
LATOYA: *(Screams.)* Actually, that's kinda fun. *(Screams.)*
EMMA: Let's all three try it. One, two ... *(ALL scream.)*
LATOYA: Oh, that felt so good. Once more. *(ALL scream.)*
YOKO: Now. I feel like a different person.
EMMA: Me too. *(They start to leave.)*
LATOYA: You can't stop now. I'm just getting started.
EMMA: I gotta go. My mom's waiting for me.
YOKO: Me too.
LATOYA: This isn't fair.
EMMA: Whoever said ...
YOKO: Life was fair.
EMMA and YOKO: *(Scream.)* Bye, now. Have a nice day. *(Exit.)*
LATOYA: *(Screams long and loud.)*

Millennia: The Search for Meaning

(Girls in pajamas, snacking, chatting)

NANCY: *(Pouring soda)* OK, girlfriends. Eat, drink and be merry.

MOIRA: For tomorrow, we graduate.

ALL: *(Cheers, whistles, etc.)*

DIDI: A toast.

KIT: To the end of a twelve-year depression.

ALL: *(Cheers, etc.)*

DIDI: To the future.

ALL: *(Ad libs, cheers, ALL drink.)*

KIT: To the new millennia. Rah rah.

MOIRA: And to us, the generation who will shape it.

NANCY: Tomorrow night, we walk, in cap and gown, into a new paradigm. Life after high school.

KIT: The question is, is there life after high school?

MOIRA: I suppose someone will now go all philosophical on us about the challenges ahead, and all that idiocy.

DIDI: Kit's giving the Valedictorian speech.

NANCY: To the Valedictorian.

ALL: *(Toasting, cheers, ad libs)*

MOIRA: You've been very secretive about your big speech. It must be awfully good.

KIT: I haven't written it yet.

NANCY: You lie. Come clean. What's it all about? What's your vision for the twenty-first century? We won't laugh.

MOIRA: We might even like it.

KIT: You won't. So, Nancy. When are you going off to college? Did you give up on summer school?

NANCY: Yep. Decided to spend my last free summer doing good

works in Mexico. I'm going down on a Habitat for Humanity gig.

KIT: How humanitarian.

NANCY: Yeah. Once school starts, that's it for the rest of my life. Four years college, three years law school. It seems like forever.

DIDI: You'll be a great lawyer.

NANCY: I hope. I've always thought there was something beautiful about the law, ever since I was a kid, when my dad started teaching me about the "laws" of our family. It's like it's this invisible web, holding us, society, together. I like that, and want to be part of it. What about you, Moira? Got any plans yet?

MOIRA: I thought you'd never ask. Guess what?

DIDI: What?

MOIRA: Guess.

KIT: You won the lottery.

MOIRA: I wish.

DIDI: You're going to college after all?

MOIRA: You know how I hate school.

NANCY: You got a job.

MOIRA: Gregory and I are getting married.

ALL: *(Silence)*

MOIRA: Don't everybody talk at once.

KIT: Married?

NANCY: When? When are you getting married?

MOIRA: We got engaged over the weekend, but I haven't even told my parents. I wanted to tell you, my best friends, first. And I want you all to be in the wedding. My bridesmaids.

NANCY: When? I might be in Mexico.

MOIRA: Isn't anybody going to congratulate me?

DIDI: I guess, if that's what you want.

MOIRA: Gregory's being transferred out of state, so we decided to get married. We don't want to be apart. I guess we're really in love.

KIT: You aren't ... are you?

NANCY: Oh, Kit. Don't be such a cynic.

KIT: Just thought I'd ask. Somebody has to or we won't make it through the night, we'll all be so busy wondering. I suppose you're going to do the whole housewife bit, with window treatments and all that jazz.

MOIRA: Oh, I can hardly wait. And you will have to wear pink, if you're going to be in the wedding. All of you will.

NANCY: So when is this life-changing event? I'm going to Mexico, remember?

MOIRA: The last week in June. I want to be a June bride. And his new job starts July first. Our honeymoon will be the journey from here to there. Isn't that romantic?

DIDI: I can't make the wedding. I'll be leaving soon.

NANCY: Where are you going?

DIDI: I've joined the Marine Corps.

ALL: *(Silence)*

DIDI: Well, somebody say something.

KIT: People named Didi do not join the Marine Corps.

DIDI: Well, I did. And I'm leaving in two weeks. Wanna come? They're looking for a few more good women.

MOIRA: Then you won't be in my wedding. You won't even be here.

DIDI: Nope. I'll be at boot camp.

KIT: Learning to kill your fellow humans.

DIDI: I'll be learning how to salute, and march and make up a bunk.

NANCY: I can't believe you joined the Marines. You don't even like war movies. Why'd you do it?

DIDI: So I can eventually go to college on the GI bill. You know my parents can't afford to send me. And if I take out all those loans, I'll spend the rest of my life paying it all off.

MOIRA: Will you have to kill people?

DIDI: I hope not. But if I have to, I guess I will.

MOIRA: Kit, I hope you'll at least be here for my wedding.

KIT: Afraid not.

NANCY: Where are you off to?

KIT: My aunt is taking me on a world tour.

NANCY: You're going to Europe? To wander around in all those creepy castles. Oooh! You can have a continental romance.

MOIRA: You're my best friends. Who'll walk with me, down the aisle?

KIT: Wait till Didi gets out of boot camp. She can goose step to the altar in her pink camouflage suit.

DIDI: You can make fun, but I'm excited about it. I think being a

Marine is neat. And think of all the great guys I'll meet. I may even marry a general. Wouldn't that be something? I just hope I don't ever have to really fight. Like in a real war. But they don't have those very much anymore, do they?

KIT: Didi, if you're going to be a warrior, fight fiercely. Nobody wants a wimp defending the country.

MOIRA: Oh, stop it. Didi could never kill anybody.

NANCY: Everybody could, if they have to. Even you, Moira.

MOIRA: I knew this would happen.

KIT: What? Us having a meaningful discussion about life and death?

MOIRA: Everybody going in different directions. We'll never see each other again. Oh, we'll all have great lives, I'm sure, but it'll never be the same. We have to promise to get together every year, and stay in touch with each other.

NANCY: A toast. To us. Forever and ever.

ALL: *(Cheers, ad libs, etc.)*

DIDI: Kit, you've never been any place in your whole life, except the grocery store. A world tour? Give me a break. I see you kayaking down the rapids, not castles in Europe.

KIT: We're going to the Amazon.

DIDI: Amazon what? Dot com?

NANCY: The Amazon River, dummy.

MOIRA: The Amazon? Why?

KIT: We're going to see the rain forest before it's burned away. And to the Galapagos Islands, to see all the animals. We'll take an ice breaker in Antarctica to see the penguins, and to Australia to see the Koalas before they all die out. Then we're going to China. If we get lucky, we'll see a wild panda. There's a few tigers left in India, and some snow leopards in Ethiopia. Of course, we'll go to Kenya, to see the elephants. We'll fly to the North Pole. I want to see the polar bears before global warming melts all the ice and the bears go the way of the spotted owl. I think we're going to Russia, too, and any place else we think of, where animals still have a natural habitat. We'll be gone at least a year. Maybe more. As long as it takes. My aunt's very rich.

MOIRA: I'm stunned.

DIDI: I'm jealous.

NANCY: I want to go. How'd this trip come about anyway?

KIT: I was going over my Valedictorian speech with my aunt, so she invited me to go in search of the natural world, while it still exists. And yes, you can come. And Moira, you are ... aren't you?

NANCY: Didn't we have this discussion?

DIDI: What's the speech about, Kit? You have to tell us now.

NANCY: C'mon. You can't hold out after this revelation.

KIT: If Moira won't tell, why should I?

NANCY: Moira, are you? *(Silence)*

MOIRA: We were going to get married anyway. This just hastens things along.

DIDI: I think it's wonderful. Congratulations. I'm very happy for you.

MOIRA: Thanks. I'm happy too. I've always wanted a baby, and now I'll get one. Just a bit sooner than expected, but that's fine with me.

NANCY: Stop. Everything's going so fast. Now Moira's going maternal, Kit's going to the ends of the earth, Didi's going militaristic and I feel like I'm just going. Like my whole life is coming to an end.

DIDI: It is. High school's over. New paradigm ... the great big outside world. Now Kit, what's the speech about? You promised.

KIT: OK. But you won't like it.

MOIRA: Tell us anyway.

KIT: Remember all those discussions we had in science, about global warming, and the hole in the ozone, and pollution and endangered species. Well, it's one thing to study it, but another to speak out. I feel I have to speak out. Look, you really don't want to go into this now, do you?

MOIRA: Of course we do.

NANCY: Spit it out. We can handle. it.

KIT: OK. You asked for it. I call my speech, *(Pause)* Millennia, The Search for Meaning in a Dying World. *(Silence)* I told you.

MOIRA: You're right. I hate it.

DIDI: Sounds like a sci-fi novel.

NANCY: I'm impressed. Now, tomorrow night, after graduation, we're all going out to The Cave to dance the night away, right?

KIT: Right. We live on a dying planet, so let's all go dancing.

NANCY: Why not? The world won't care. And we might have a good time.

DIDI: Let's have a toast. To Moira. And her baby.

KIT: Right. Bringing a baby into a dying world. What gives you the right, Moira?

MOIRA: Right? What right? It's natural. Women have babies. Since the beginning of time, we fall in love, and have babies, and that's what life is all about.

KIT: Maybe in the old paradigm. Not the new one. And I say so, in my speech.

MOIRA: You're way out of line on this, Kit. I'm going to tell the principal what you're planning. He'll stop you.

KIT: I'm the Valedictorian. It's my speech, and I can say what I want.

MOIRA: Fine. But I don't have to listen.

KIT: That's right. Denial. The curse of the afflicted.

MOIRA: I hate this. I just hate it. If this is the new paradigm, count me out. Everybody's getting so weird. Joining the Marines. Learning how to kill people. Going ballistic about the environment. If this is life after high school, take me back. Take me back, take me back.

KIT: That's right, Moira. Run. Run away from reality, from hard truth. Nobody in their right mind should bring a baby into this dying world. But in typical selfish fashion, you and everybody else will just keep on multiplying like rabbits till every living thing on the planet is dead. So, cheers. To Moira and her baby.

MOIRA: *(Slaps KIT's face. KIT throws her drink into MOIRA's face. Deep silence.)*

NANCY: I think we should all take a deep breath.

MOIRA: I think Kit should shut up and leave.

DIDI: Maybe we should just go to sleep. This is a slumber party.

NANCY: This is supposed to be a fun evening. So, our lives are changing. And the world's changing. Whatever. We'll deal with it. But this may be the last time we're all together, for a long, long time. So, let's have a toast. To me, to higher education. To Didi and her rifle. To Kit and her journey. To Moira, and her new baby. *(Silence)*

DIDI: Nancy's right. The future is up for grabs. All we have is now. Us. So, here's to us. To friendship. To Nancy, peacemaker, diplomat. A great future awaits you, girlfriend. We're gonna see you soon sitting on the Supreme Court, swinging with the Supremes. All right! *(NANCY and DIDI drink.)*

NANCY: To Didi. Warrior woman, friend. And that General, just waiting to be found. *(NANCY and DIDI drink. Silence)* Listen, everybody. We've all been friends too long to break up now. We've had good times and bad all through school. What made it bearable? Us. The four of us. Holding tight. So, you two. C'mon, Kiss and make up. Kit? Moira? You can't throw away years of friendship. You just can't. If you do, the world as we know it, really does come to an end. Nobody wants that. *(Silence)*

MOIRA: To Kit, who wouldn't get so passionate if you didn't really care. I love that about you, Kit, even if it drives me nuts. So, here's to a safe journey and a joyful return home. *(All drink.)*

NANCY: Kit? *(Silence)*

DIDI: C'mon, Kit. Give it up. *(Silence)*

MOIRA: Let her go. It's all right. *(Silence)* I think I better leave. *(Silence)*

KIT: No. Don't go. Actually, Moira, I'm glad you're having a baby. Babies are symbols of hope. I know it'll be the most beautiful, most magical baby in the world. And you'll be a great mom. A great, great mom. *(They hug. NANCY and DIDI join them in a group embrace.)*

KIT: So, little mama. Is this where the baby is? Is it kicking yet? *(Puts hand on MOIRA's stomach.)*

DIDI: I want to feel too. *(Puts hands on MOIRA's stomach.)*

NANCY: You know how I hate to be left out. *(Puts hands on MOIRA's stomach.)*

MOIRA: *(Puts her hands on top of all the others.)* Since I can't get you to be my bridesmaids, I'm making you all my baby's godmothers.

NANCY: Good. Now we really do have to stay together, don't we?

ALL: *(Cheers, ad libs, etc.)*

About the Author

I grew up in a big house on a corner, in a small town in Louisiana, where, after many wanderings across the globe, I live today. On the same corner.

I love being a theatre artist, because to me, theatre is one of the few places I know where everybody wins. The actors have a wonderful time rehearsing and then giving the play away to the audience. The audience has a wonderful time. Engaged by the players, they lose themselves in the play.

As a playwright, I love the idea that, while I live in my little corner of the world, I'm connected through my plays, to people all around the globe. The young woman in Yellow Knife, Ontario. A student in Belgium. Recovering addicts in a rehab center in South Carolina. The girl in Holland, playing her part in Dutch. Audiences, sitting in the dark, lost in the magic of theatre. Through my words, they come to know something more about me. We're connected, in a very real, and wonderful way. We're neighbors, in the global village.

Now, you will know something of me, through these *Scenes and Monologs for Young Women*. For I am all the parts, as are you.

Maya Levy

Order Form

Meriwether Publishing Ltd.
P.O. Box 7710
Colorado Springs, CO 80933
Telephone: (719) 594-4422

Please send me the following books:

________	**Acting Scenes and Monologs for Young Women #BK-B228** **by Maya Levy** *A collection of monologs and scenes for young women*	**$14.95**
________	**The Flip Side #BK-B221** **by Heather H. Henderson** *64 point-of-view monologs for teens*	**$12.95**
________	**Acting Natural #BK-B133** **by Peg Kehret** *Honest-to-life monologs, dialogs, and playlets for teens*	**$14.95**
________	**Winning Monologs for Young Actors #BK-B127** **by Peg Kehret** *Honest-to-life monologs for young actors*	**$14.95**
________	**Encore! More Winning Monologs for Young Actors #BK-B144** **by Peg Kehret** *More honest-to-life monologs for young actors*	**$14.95**
________	**Spotlight #BK-B176** **by Stephanie S. Fairbanks** *Solo scenes for student actors*	**$12.95**
________	**Get in the Act! #BK-B104** **by Shirley Ullom** *Monologs, dialogs, and skits for teens*	**$12.95**

These and other fine Meriwether Publishing books are available at your local bookstore or direct from the publisher. Use the handy order form on this page.

Name: ____

Organization name: ______________________________

Address: ____

City: ______________________________ State: ____________

Zip: ____________________ Phone: ____________________

❑ **Check Enclosed**

❑ **Visa or MasterCard #** ______________________________

Signature: ____________________________ *Expiration Date:* ______________

(required for Visa/MasterCard orders)

COLORADO RESIDENTS: Please add 3% sales tax.
SHIPPING: Include $2.75 for the first book and 50¢ for each additional book ordered.

❑ *Please send me a copy of your complete catalog of books and plays.*